PLAY
FOR
SOMETHING

Malte Kramer

 **PETERSON'S**®

About Peterson's®

Peterson's® provides the accurate, dependable, high-quality education content and guidance you need to succeed. No matter where you are on your academic or professional path, you can rely on Peterson's publications and its online information at **www.petersons.com** for the most up-to-date education exploration data, expert test-prep tools, and top-notch career success resources—everything you need to achieve your goals.

For more information, contact Peterson's, 3 Columbia Circle, Albany, NY 12203–5158; 800-338-3282 Ext. 54229; or find us online at **www.petersons.com**.

ISBN: 978-0-7689-4112-8

Printed in the United States

10 9 8 7 6 5 4 3 2 1   18 17 16

First Edition

Dedication:

To all my former teammates: I wrote this book for you.

TABLE OF CONTENTS

FOREWORD

I first met Malte when we were both asked to speak to a class of freshman student-athletes about the trials and tribulations that they would be facing as they entered the collegiate ranks. While listening to Malte, I had no idea that he was a valedictorian! He was extremely well spoken, but his relaxed nature was not what I would have expected from a "brainiac." As I continued listening to Malte, it blew my mind that someone could be so laid-back (t-shirt, shorts, and flip-flops) yet be a student-athlete with top-of-class honors—all at the same time!

In *Play for Something*, Malte Kramer has nailed it right on the head! This is an ABSOLUTE MUST-READ for any student-athlete in high school or college (and pros for that matter). Malte was a valedictorian, so he speaks from a place of absolute knowledge and understanding. I anticipated that this might be a difficult read and maybe even a bit stuffy coming from such an educated young man. But, to Malte's credit, his relaxed, informational, straightforward, and honest approach drew me in, and I couldn't put this book down! I so wish *Play for Something* had been available when I was in school because it made me realize just how easy studying can be. With tips like batching, Parkinson's Law, and the 80/20 rule, student-athletes will see how they can study, practice, have fun, and flourish all at the same time! At the end of each section there is a helpful SUMMARY, which focuses on the main points. Malte also equips with you tips and strategies to help you overcome everything from fear to procrastination. If you are a student-athlete, I highly recommend—NO, I insist—that you read this book as there is something for EVERYONE! Malte is "paying it forward" so LISTEN UP!

Enjoy!

Doug Christie

Former NBA Player, Sacramento Kings, 3-time NBA All Defensive Team

INTRODUCTION

I wouldn't waste your time. If I did, I would be going against one of my own key principles presented in this book: use time consciously. Therefore, if you already know why you should read this book, and why I am the right person to have written it for you, go ahead and skip this introduction.

My name is Malte Kramer. I recently graduated as the valedictorian from Pepperdine University—while playing NCAA Division I basketball on a full scholarship. Simply put, I know how to play in front of thousands on Tuesday and ace a final on Wednesday. I finished with a 4.0 GPA. That means in four years of college I did not receive a grade lower than an A. No, not even an A-.

My journey began in 2010 when I came to America to play basketball while working toward a college degree. I was neither athletic nor talented enough to earn a scholarship to a four-year school. I went to Cuesta Community College in San Luis Obispo, California, paying the out-of-state tuition with my own money. Just a few years later, I was the valedictorian at a prestigious school with an acceptance letter from Stanford Graduate School of Business in my hands.

Along the way, I tried countless strategies, figured out what didn't work, refined what did, and developed a system that allowed me to achieve unparalleled results. This book contains uncommon approaches, effective shortcuts, and alternative ways of thinking. Moreover, I supplemented my own findings with those of extremely successful student-athletes and experts from all over the globe. I interviewed Olympians, business executives, Academic All-Americans, college valedictorians, and professional athletes. I took courses in speed-reading, learned from a memory world champion, and read countless books on self-development, education, and psychology. My hope is that this book will help you realize your dreams.

I've been called a genius, but never by anyone who really knows me. People who don't know me tend to assume that I must be either freakishly intelligent or lacking any kind of social life, a basketball-playing Einstein or a loner who lives with his books. They're wrong on all accounts. I don't have any gifts that you don't have, like seeing numbers as colors or a photographic memory. And I didn't give up my social life in college either. The truth is, I spent more time exploring Malibu beaches and the LA nightlife than many of my teammates. I made great friends, dated lots of girls, and did all the things one should in college. I could tell you stories, but then this book would probably never get published. Worse, it might be deemed inappropriate reading for student-athletes.

If you're a student-athlete, I can relate to you. I was in your shoes for the last four years of my life. I've been through the 5 a.m. workouts, the losing streaks, and the fights with teammates, and I know what it feels like to be benched. I had to battle back from knee surgery by spending 3 hours in the training room every damn day, on top of the regular team practice regimen. I know the disappointment of a close loss and the feeling after a big win—like you're on top of the world. I still hear the squeaking of the sneakers when I go to sleep. And when people ask me what I do, I still feel the urge to answer: "I'm a basketball player." So if you're worried about this book not being applicable to you, let me put your mind at ease. I am just like you, with a slight difference: I know how to win at academics.

So what prompted me to write this book? In a word: teammates. I've had more than 100 over the years, and many of them are now my best friends. The number of good people I have had the fortune to be around is nothing short of amazing. And yet, I see so many of them struggling with life away from basketball. Many of my former teammates make more dumb decisions than free throws. One got caught drinking on a dry campus and was suspended. One became academically ineligible because he forgot an assignment. One lost his scholarship because he couldn't pass a general education course. One didn't know how to manage his money and ended up broke after an 8-year professional career in Europe and was forced to move back in with his mom. I've seen people who are smarter than I am fail; I've seen better athletes end up nowhere. Many times I have thought that these failures could be prevented. This book will provide you with the knowledge that you won't get during freshman seminar. I will give it to you straight. This will enable you to overcome the obstacles you will face as a student-athlete.

FAQ:

If you're not a genius, how did you become valedictorian?

By using a mindset, a skill set, and a number of strategies that can be learned.

Can I develop and use them?

Absolutely. That's what this book is for.

Will I only get A's from now on?

That depends entirely on you. Everything you need is in this book and between your ears.

Will I stay academically eligible?

Yes, if you follow the guidelines presented in this book, you will always manage to stay academically eligible. More important, you will set yourself up for the life that is to come when your knees give out (and they eventually will, trust me).

WHAT'S AHEAD IN THIS BOOK

Here are some of the things this book will teach you:

- How to beat the educational system

- How to get a 4.0 GPA while spending 30+ hours a week on your sport

- Memory tricks to cut your study time by up to 70 percent while getting straight A's

- Speed-reading techniques to read 4 times faster while memorizing up to 3 times the material

- Test-taking strategies to crush any exam by completely getting rid of stress and anxiety

- How to secure a professional career in the future while focusing 100 percent on your sport now

- How to procrastinate the right way

- How to get an A on every essay in half the writing time by using a simple template

- Advanced memory techniques used by memory champions to remember over 22,000 digits in order

- Five ways to find your true inspiration

- How to prepare now for high income and happiness after you retire from your sport

- How to inspire others, become a better person, and live a happy life

PART I: INSPIRATION AND VISION

CHAPTER 1:
THE FOUNDATION

When gymnast Elfi Schlegel arrived at the University of Florida in 1983, she had been a member of the Canadian national gymnastics team for seven years and had competed in the Olympics three years prior. At the age of 18, she was already a star in the world of gymnastics. She had every reason to focus on nothing but her sport. After all, "I was training for the Olympics" is a pretty good excuse for not turning in your homework. And yet, that's not what she did.

Elfi became an Academic All-American in her sophomore year. She graduated with a degree in telecommunications and went on to become arguably the most recognized sports reporter in the field of gymnastics. She left a legacy not just as an athlete but as a professional. In 2013, she was inducted into the Academic All-American Hall of Fame.

When talking to Elfi you get the sense that the answers are obvious, because in a way they are. When I asked her why she worked so hard in the classroom, she explained: "There was such pride in coming from a country that they didn't recruit. I felt a sense of responsibility and a sense of pride toward my country, and I did not want to mess up." When asked how she dealt with the distractions at a large university, she said: "I did not sign up to become the best partier. That wasn't my lifestyle. There was no time." And when I inquired about the reason for choosing the University of Florida, she named the strength of their journalism program and her wish to work as a broadcaster one day.

Elfi not only took pride in performing at the highest level, she also had goals beyond her athletic career. Whatever your background may be, success starts with knowing *where* you want to go and *why*. Without a vision, you're a ship with no direction. While it's possible to stumble across your life's calling, more often than not you will drown.

So how did Elfi do it? The short answer is that she found a unique blend of strategies and motivation that worked for her. The truth is there isn't a single piece of advice anyone can give you that will turn you from failure to success. It's a combination of things that will allow you to excel. No matter what people tell you about success, usually their advice can be categorized into answers to these three questions:

Why?

What?

How?

Without the answers to all of these questions, you are unlikely to succeed. Elfi had clear answers to each of the questions, whether she knew it at the time or not.

First you have to know *why* you should even consider doing something and *why* it's worth your time. This can't be some vague idea; you need a strong conviction and purpose in order to fuel your ambition. Anything that relates to your motivation, inspiration, and goals answers the question of *why*? There are countless reasons for striving to become exceptional outside of your sport. The five most common ones are: professional goals, personal reasons, competitive drive, intellectual pride, and a realistic outlook. The first part of this book will deal with these reasons extensively and help you develop your own. It all starts with harvesting the inspiration that got you here in the first place.

Next you have to learn specifically *what* it will take, *what* you have to sacrifice, and *what* you have to put in place to be successful. You need strategies, processes, and systems that will support your quest for success in school and, more importantly, life. The second part of the book is devoted to the knowledge and systems that will allow you to achieve the goals you have set for yourself.

Finally, you need to learn how to apply these strategies to your life. Knowledge is useless without the know-how needed to put it in action. The third and final part of this book provides you with the *how-to* tips and tricks and practical tools you can immediately put into action in your studies.

SUMMARY

- Successful people know *what* they need to do, *how* to do it, and *why* they should do it.
- The *why* consists of inspiration and motivation, the *what* involves systems and behaviors, and the *how* includes practical skills and tricks.
- The five most common reasons for wanting to excel off the field are:
    1. Professional goals
    2. Personal reasons
    3. Competitive drive
    4. Intellectual pride
    5. A realistic outlook

"A goal without a plan is just a wish."

—*Antoine de Saint-Exupery*

CHAPTER 2:
TAKING A PAGE
FROM LEBRON JAMES

In 2012, LeBron James was facing the type of pressure that would cause most men to break. Having left the Cleveland Cavaliers to join forces with Dwayne Wade and Chris Bosh in Miami, he had become the NBA's number one villain. Moreover, the year before, his team had lost to a Dallas Mavericks ensemble of 35-year-olds who lacked star power. James had been unable to perform when it mattered, choking in crucial games and disappearing in the fourth quarter. He was the laughingstock of the NBA, nicknamed "Le Choke," and experts agreed that while a gifted player, he lacked the killer instincts and "winner gene" of a Kobe Bryant or Michael Jordan.

Now, one year later, it was his chance, maybe his last, to prove to the world that he deserved to be called an all-time great, one of the rare players capable of putting a team on his back with a championship on the line. Everyone expected him to break again under the enormous pressure—but James delivered. His team routed Oklahoma 4 games to 1 on the way to a title, and James was named the finals MVP after an outstanding play-off performance that eliminated any doubt of his ability to perform in the clutch. Not only did he deliver one incredible performance after another but his demeanor had changed drastically, too. He didn't show off, trash talk, or celebrate extensively; instead he appeared focused and at ease while letting his game do the talking. It was obvious that he had matured and taken his mental game to the next level.

What many people don't know is the changes James made to get there. He developed an obsession with books and publicly credited reading for making him calmer during the playoffs. The most dominant player of his generation had realized the power of personal growth and mental strength through reading. He didn't care about looking cool; instead, he found what worked for him. He took pride, not just in his physical abilities but in his mental toughness. Photos showed James reading before and after games, essentially turning his locker stall into a library. What made his new passion all the more fascinating was the selection of books he was devouring. ESPN reported that he was reading everything from biographies to fiction, from history to bestsellers, from classics to books about human psychology.

EXERCISE

Go to a book store and look for books in different sections. What kind of books spark your interest? Make a list of ten books you want to read. Buy one and read 10 pages each night until you finish it. Then buy the next book on the list—or to save a little money, visit your local library and borrow the books.

_____   _____

_____   _____

_____   _____

_____   _____

_____   _____

James' story is not a single case. Most top athletes realize at some point in their careers that in order to reach the next level of mental strength, they need to grow intellectually. That's usually when they start to focus on controlling their thoughts and developing a strong mind. In contrast to the best professional athletes, many student-athletes don't care about learning or intellectual growth. It takes them years to figure out that by embracing personal and intellectual growth, they can reach heights they never even dreamed of. The following pages are aimed at shortening that learning curve while accelerating personal growth.

SUMMARY

- Personal growth entails intellectual growth.

- Elite athletes typically train their minds as well as their bodies.

- Reading is an excellent way to stimulate intellectual growth.

"As much as we pump iron and we run to build our strength up, we need to build our mental strength up … so we can focus … so we can be in concert with one another."

—Coach Phil Jackson

CHAPTER 3:
INTELLECTUAL PRIDE

Most coaches emphasize pride as one of the key characteristics of success: pride in winning, pride in competing, pride in protecting the home court, pride in earning respect, and pride in being taken seriously. Athletes embrace that thinking on the court. However, when it comes to academics, a professional career, and life, many student-athletes don't have any pride at all. How else would you explain why so many fail as soon as their athletic careers come to an end?

Think about it this way: If you're getting scored on every time down the court, it means you lack defensive pride. If you barely pass your classes, it means you lack intellectual pride. Put simply, you're being told every day that you are underperforming intellectually. And you do nothing about it. It's like every day someone dunks on you, and you just stand there with his junk in your face. As an athlete you would feel ashamed. Your coach would call you a disgrace to the program or some other suitable insult. And he or she would be right.

In your professional career, most of you won't have the coach who is going to tell you that your performance off the court is a disgrace to your potential, to your opportunity, to your scholarship, and, frankly, to every kid who wishes he or she had access to the education you have. So you have to do that yourself. It's about making a decision to take responsibility, to not accept mediocrity anymore, and to grow as a person every day.

EXERCISE

- Write down your current GPA.

  _____

- Write down what you think your GPA would be if you gave academics your best effort.

  _____

One phrase that I heard over and over from my coaches was "Are you the hammer or the nail?" On the court we all embrace that sort of thinking, but what about in the classroom, in our career, in life? Ask yourself if you have ever dominated life apart from your sport. In other words, have you ever been so good at a skill, a task, or an assignment that no one could touch you? This sort of excellence and competence will allow you to excel in school and the professional world when your athletic career ends. As soon as you start taking pride in your intellectual competence, you won't accept a 2.0 GPA, or not being able to write properly, or not being able to remember things—because accepting those things means you're losing every day.

SUMMARY

- As an athlete, you earn respect by taking pride in your athletic performance. As a professional, you earn respect by taking pride in your professional performance.

- There are millions of people who would kill to be in your position.

- Be grateful and don't squander the opportunities you have.

- There is only one way to stop underperforming intellectually: take responsibility and show pride in your work off the field.

"Most people fail because they trade what they want most, for what they want at the moment."

—*Unknown*

CHAPTER 4: COMPETITIVE DRIVE

Michael Jordan once lost a recreational game of table tennis to a teammate. He immediately got his own table and practiced every day for the next six months. He won the rematch. The takeaway of this anecdote is not just that Jordan was hyper-competitive but also that his competitiveness reached beyond the basketball court. He did not just compete on the court but at everything he did.

Most high-performance athletes display competitive drive in their sport, but very few exhibit Jordan-like behavior in other aspects of their lives. Those who do excel. Beau Levesque, an Academic All-American who is now playing basketball professionally in Spain, credits competitive drive for his success:

> *I've often been viewed as overly competitive, especially at a young age. For as long as I can remember, I always wanted to get the top score on every test or paper because I didn't want to feel like someone knew the material better or performed on the test better than I did. I wish it had been a philosophical quest for knowledge that kept me motivated for academic success, but most of the time I saw it as a competition between the material and me or my classmates and me.*

If you are a successful student-athlete, chances are you already embrace competition on the court. It's what helps you endure endless hours of practices, early-morning conditioning workouts, and mind-numbing video sessions. You might not enjoy everything you do to be successful in your sport, but you do it anyway because, at the end of the day, you care about winning. This exact mindset is all you need to succeed in life. You have the most powerful tools at your disposal: your athlete's mindset and the determination, pride, and passion that come with it.

Unfortunately, most athletes never learn how to apply their mindset to areas outside of their sport. Those who do usually take off and never look back. Thomas Van Der Mars, an NCAA Division I basketball player and Academic All-American, who completed his master's in business degree with a 4.0 GPA, told me:

> For a long time now, I have realized that I am facing competition from everyone who seeks to pursue the same career opportunities as I do. Whether this is on or off the court, this realization made me somewhat fearful of being average or being lost in the crowd. That fear drove me to work really hard.

The fear of being average and the determination to do whatever it takes to win is what has allowed athletes like Kobe Bryant, Serena Williams, and Michael Phelps to dominate. The same competitive drive has given rise to countless self-made millionaires and highly successful business leaders. Mark Cuban's reply to young entrepreneurs trying to compete with him? "I just love to kick your ass! You know, seriously, I'm just so competitive that, you know, f**k y'all. I want to win and that's it in a nutshell."

SUMMARY

- Successful athletes care about winning, and their determination, pride, and passion are what later help them succeed in life.

- The fear of being average and the determination to do whatever it takes to win is what has enabled top athletes to dominate and has given rise to countless self-made millionaires and highly successful business leaders.

- Compete like Jordan, develop a Cuban attitude, and apply your competitiveness off the court.

"Men lie, women lie, numbers don't."

—*Jay Z*

CHAPTER 5:
LIFE'S STAT SHEET—
A REALISTIC OUTLOOK

You use stats to interpret your game, right? Let's use stats to interpret your future.

Most underperforming student-athletes give one of two reasons for their lack of academic effort and pride:

1. "I think I have a good chance of going pro. That's all I am focused on; everything else is a distraction."

2. "I don't think my grades really make a difference. As long as I graduate, I will be fine."

Both of these statements are myths. Don't believe me? Let's take a look at the numbers.

The Going-Pro Myth

If you're an NCAA athlete, your chances of going pro are somewhere between 0.8 percent and 1.5 percent on average, depending on your sport. That means if you're not absolutely killing it, you won't go pro. It sounds harsh, but that's the reality.

Most athletes want to go pro, not just because of their love of the game, but also for external reasons like fame and money. It's perfectly okay to want those things, but betting your entire life on the 1.5 percent chance of going pro is foolish. If you had to bet your life savings at a roulette table, you wouldn't put it all on one number. Instead you would bet some on black and some on red to make sure you end up with at least something in your pocket.

It's hard for college athletes to accept the numbers because we're used to beating the odds. The thinking goes like this: We made it from high school to college; we beat the odds there, so why shouldn't we be able to do it again? Besides, we're conditioned not to doubt ourselves. We're trained to have full confidence in our ability because that helps us perform at a higher level. In addition, most of us come from a community of supporters who tell us every day how great we are. We feel special, so beating the odds doesn't seem so hard. We're told every day: If you don't believe it you won't achieve it. To reach plan A, most of us neglect plan B—and when we realize that we need it, it's often too late.

However, some of us do make it. Let's say you're one of the lucky few. You beat the odds and turn pro. You play and, depending on your sport and health, your career ends somewhere in your thirties. That means you have another 40 years or so left to work. Looking at your whole life, it's not even halftime yet. Unless you make millions and invest those well, you will need to get another job at some point. Keep in mind that you're now behind the rest of your graduating class by ten to fifteen years, with no relevant work experience. If these stats don't prompt you to take your life apart from athletics seriously, talk to a former pro and ask them about their transition into the workforce. I can almost guarantee you it sucked.

EXERCISE

Write down the answers to the following questions:

- Are you planning on playing your sport professionally?

  _____

- If so, how much money do you expect to make per year?

  _____

- How many years do you expect to play?

  _____

- Multiply your expected salary per year times the number of years you expect to play.

  _____

- Now divide that number by 50.

  _____

  That's an estimation of the amount you will have available per year for the rest of your life if you only make money playing your sport (not considering taxes).

- Is that enough to enable you to live your dream life?

  _____

The GPA Myth

A recent WallStreetOasis.com[1] study on compensation in investment banking concluded that GPA significantly influences salary. Based on the responses of over 3,400 employees of large and small investment banking firms who voluntarily reported their pay to the website, on average, third-year analysts earned a total compensation of $65,000 if their GPA was 2.8 or less, compared to $77,700 for a GPA of 2.9 to 3.1 and $115,700 for a GPA of 3.8 to 4.0.

> **A- students made over $50,000 more per year than C-students.**

The study also found a strong correlation between undergraduate grades earned and associates' salaries. A first-year associate in investment banking, the study concluded, pulled in an average of $79,700 if his or her GPA was 2.9 to 3.1 and $99,700 for a GPA of 3.2 to 3.4—a full $20,000 premium. Just a slightly higher GPA, 3.5 to 3.7, was shown to increase total pay to $137,400.

> **Going from a 2.9 GPA to a 3.5 GPA in college increased average yearly salary by almost $60,000!**

It's hard to argue with these numbers, and they can be eye opening. However, to be motivated to get better as a student and person every day, you have to find your personal *why*. That's what the next chapter is about.

---

1. http://www.businessinsider.com/could-your-gpa-predict-your-income-2014-4?IR=T&r=US&IR=T

SUMMARY

- Your academic performance matters.

- Your chances of going pro are very slim.

- There is a strong correlation between your GPA and the salary you will receive later on.

"**Somewhere** behind the athlete you've become and the hours of the practice and the coaches who have pushed you is a little girl who fell in love with the game and never looked back ... play for her."

—*Mia Hamm, award-winning professional soccer player*

CHAPTER 6:
TRUE INSPIRATION

The rational approach clearly shows why working hard apart from basketball is worth it. However, for most of us, understanding something rationally and being able to apply it every day are two entirely different challenges. With only a rational understanding of why I should succeed apart from basketball, I would have never developed the drive needed to get to where I am today. The real reason that will end up driving you to success is your personal *why*. It's the fundamental explanation for what drives you. It's the underlying motivation for your work. It's not rational, and it's unique to every person. It's a feeling, a fear, a worldview, an emotional connection, or a relationship.

EXERCISE

Take a piece of paper, or use the lines below, and write down your *why*. What is it that drives you to work hard in your sport? Is there something or someone you think of when times get tough to help you keep going?

_____

_____

_____

_____

_____

Virtually every one of the successful student-athletes I interviewed had an inspiring personal story that explained their drive and motivation. Out of the many incredible stories, Beau Levesque's stood out. The Academic All-American and professional basketball player shared the following:

Athletically, my little cousin Alex is my inspiration. When he was 3, he fell victim to a disease that took all the feeling out of his hands and feet and made it impossible for him to gain weight. Right now, at 21 years old, he is about 5 feet tall and weighs only 50 pounds. Despite all of this, he is one of the most positive, light-hearted people I know. I have used him for motivation and inspiration so much in my life because he makes me realize how truly blessed I am to be playing the sport I love. Countless times, but especially in the mile test at Saint Mary's, I would think to myself, 'Imagine how hard Alex would run this mile if he could trade places with me for one day! Would he quit when he gets tired?' Without even knowing it, he has given me strength in some of my hardest times physically. Before my last two seasons at Saint Mary's, we came up with a saying, either 'My Talent Your Heart' or 'Your Talent My Heart.' Before every game he would text me, 'YTMH,' and I would always respond by saying 'MTYH'."

Often the most important people in our lives are the ones that inspire us to dream bigger and to work harder. My inspiration comes from my grandfather. He was a professional soccer player who competed for Germany in the Olympics in 1928. After retiring from professional soccer, he studied to become a doctor and a few years later opened a hospital for women. Whenever we went to visit him, he played soccer with me in the backyard and taught me his tips and tricks. Afterward, he usually let me play in his office in between easels and paintings, large bookshelves filled with classic novels, and stacks of poems he had written over the years. He was a true Renaissance man—not content with excellence in just one arena. Even though he died when I was 6, he still left me with an appreciation for greatness and virtue. Whenever I get tired, I think of him and those memories remind me of what is possible in one's lifetime.

During my senior year at Pepperdine, our coach, Marty Wilson, asked everyone to tell their personal *why* to the entire team. For many of us it was a family member. A common answer was: "The reason why I do what I do is my mother. I want to make her proud because she raised me, and I would be nothing without her." Some said their motivation was to be a role model for younger siblings, the people in their neighborhood, or their home country. Some said the reason for their hard work was God.

Whether we realize it or not, our personal *why* is the strongest motivation we have. Most of us apply it whenever times get tough. When we are ready to quit, we think of the person, the goal, or the love that has gotten us here, and we decide to fight through. Expanding your personal reasons outside of your sport will be the most powerful step you can take to succeed. If your personal *why* is to be a role model for the kids in your neighborhood, strive to inspire them by having a meaningful career off the court as well as on the court. If your motivation comes from your mother, make her proud by graduating with honors. If your inspiration comes from God, make the most of the talents you've been given.

SUMMARY

- Inspiration precedes success.
- A personal *why* is oftentimes a person, but it can also be a worldview, a fear, or even God.
- Know your personal *why*, and learn to apply it outside of your sport.

"**Most** of the successful people I've known are the ones who do more listening than talking."

—*Bernard M. Baruch*

CHAPTER 7:
BEATING THE SYSTEM

There's a reason why your school is part of what's called an "educational system." It's a system because it teaches (almost) the same content year after year and awards grades based on how well you perform given the rules of the system.

Many athletes in college try fighting the system by rebelling against it, showing off how little they care while broadcasting to the world their nonconformity to the rules. It feels good and powerful to put the middle finger up especially if you're used to being "the man." Once you dominate someone on the court or field, you carry that feeling with you for the rest of your life. So when someone or something puts you down, your natural, inherent instinct is to fight back and try to win. However, most athletes figure out pretty quickly that dominating the educational system takes tireless effort, so instead they choose the easy route of not giving a f***.

The idea is: "If I don't play by your rules, you can't beat me."

Unfortunately, the system almost always wins out, your athletic merits don't matter in the job market, and you don't get hired based on swag. At some point you have to play by the rules if you want to build a professional career worthy of your accomplishments as an athlete.

EXERCISE

Think about an instance when you or one of your teammates talked back to your coach.

- Who won the argument? _____
- What was the consequence? _____
- Was it a smart decision to talk back? _____

To understand what I mean, let me give you my personal perspective. Like most athletes, I grew up with a chip on my shoulder due to the constant competition in my sport. I hated losing, and I hated looking bad. As a result, I worked harder than most and became obsessed with winning. I dressed in the coolest shoes, talked trash, and never admitted weakness. In middle school, I was a mediocre student. I only made an effort in those classes that I was naturally good in, while completely ignoring the ones that didn't come easy. I said things like: "I hate my French teacher. No way am I studying for that next test! Who cares anyway?" In high school, I realized that I was squandering my potential, and, during junior year, I made a decision. I promised myself to never choose the easy way out again just because it was convenient—not in my sport and not anywhere else in life. I finished junior year with a 3.9 GPA and after that never got a grade below an A in any class—ever!

Because college is in fact a system, the outcome can be predicted and manipulated. If you're failing, it's not by random chance but rather because you're not adapting. Remember: The only thing the system grades you on is the "set of rules" it has artificially made up over the years. As a result, if you want to be successful you have to accept and embrace those rules.

Note: Adapting does not mean giving up on your ideals or individualism; it means playing the system instead of letting it play you. Keeping your head down at the right time has nothing to do with weakness and everything to do with outsmarting the competition.

> **SUMMARY**
>
> - The system usually wins out unless you learn how to play it.
>
> - Keeping your head down at the right time isn't a sign of weakness if it means you're beating the system.
>
> - Blaming the system for your failures is an excuse.

"The key to making healthy decisions is to respect your future self. Honor him or her. Treat him or her like you would treat a friend or a loved one."

—A. J. Jacobs, American journalist, author, and lecturer

CHAPTER 8:
YOUR FUTURE

Have you ever talked to a former high school quarterback? If so I wouldn't be surprised if the conversation revolved around that one big game when he threw the game-winning pass, or that one time his team won State. Many retired athletes live in the past, because it's the best time they ever had. Their life peaked along with their career at age 20. It's often crushing when they realize that life will never ever be as good again.

EXERCISE

Imagine you couldn't play your sport anymore, starting today.

True (T) or False (F)?

_____ I would know what to do with all the extra time.

_____ I would have a clear goal for my life.

_____ I could be just as happy tomorrow as I am today.

If you are in school it means you still have the chance to change the trajectory of your future. Do you want to live the next sixty years nostalgic about the past, or do you want a life that keeps getting better? This question is crucial because the only way to create the latter is to prepare yourself for life after sports by asking yourself what kind of person you want to be and by committing to do whatever is necessary to become that person.

Stephen Lunney, NAIA Champion and a three-time Academic All-American with a 4.0 GPA, explains how he derives motivation from his vision:

> *My inspiration has always been future-me. I remember a friend won the national championship the year before we did and I was incredibly jealous. I then said to myself, almost naively, that I would be the one who people were jealous of in a year's time. I often envision myself in the future having accomplished something and I use that as my motivation to get there.*

It is possible to achieve your wildest dreams, but first you have to set a higher standard for yourself and stop limiting yourself to athletic goals. Try to imagine yourself in twenty years. Who are you going to be? A broken person who is stuck in the past or a winner who keeps moving forward? The difference is entirely up to you. You can have a fulfilling job, take care of your parents, find a passion and make it your life, own a business, travel the world, have a family (and spoil them), or settle down on some beach and surf all day. The things you want are going to remain a daydream until you make the decision to invest in becoming someone who is known for more than their athletic ability.

The key is to set goals and to chase your dreams whole-heartedly. I frequently look at luxury real estate to remind myself of what is possible. I have no means of affording a $30,000,000 home in Malibu right now, but I know I will be able to in the future. It's a way of reminding myself of my dreams and to stay hungry.

Note: Living for the future does not mean neglecting the present. You're an athlete right now, and that's important. It's just not all that you are. There doesn't have to be a limit. Give your sport everything you've got. Just don't forget who you want to be in twenty years.

FINDING YOUR CAREER

Your career will be a big part of your vision for the future. While you might want to start a family, live in a certain place or with certain people, your career is what you will spend the most time on. It's important to give it thought without being intimidated. It's becoming easier and easier to switch careers so you're not doomed, no matter where you start out. The only bad decision you can make is to be inactive and complacent. As long as you set goals and challenge yourself to find your professional calling, there are no mistakes, just lessons. There are three approaches to decide on a career:

1. Find a passion/hobby and make it your career

2. Decide on the lifestyle you want and find a career that enables it

3. Sit back and let random chance determine where you end up

Don't settle for option 3, obviously. At least make an attempt at option 1. To begin the process of finding a career or industry you are passionate about, complete the following exercise:

EXERCISE

- Think about your college classes. Is there one that you enjoy more than others? _____

- Is there any subject that you read about in your free time, whether in books or online? _____

- Do you have a hobby outside of your sport that you could potentially turn into a career? _____

Not everyone has interests that can be turned into a career. If you cannot get excited about anything other than your sport, try to find something you're good at. Oftentimes it's possible to develop a passion for something as long as you're good at it. As a last resort, it is possible to find your professional calling by deciding on the lifestyle you want and then finding a career that enables that lifestyle. For example, if you want prestige and a six-figure income and don't mind working 80-hour weeks, investment banking might be for you. If you want to work with people and get paid based on results, consider going into sales. If you want to be in charge and have a lot of responsibility along with a ton of stress, start your own business. The point here is to start thinking about what you like doing, what you are good at, and what you want your professional life to look like in terms of work hours, independence, and salary.

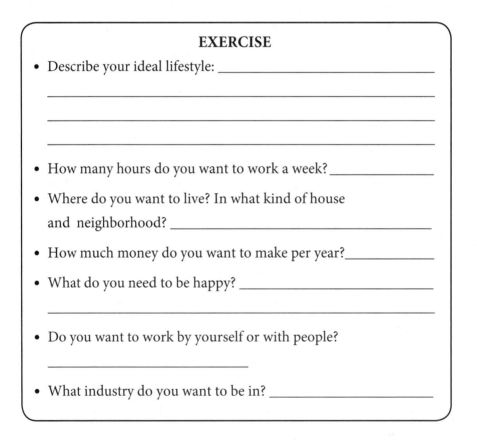

EXERCISE

- Describe your ideal lifestyle: _____
  _____
  _____
  _____

- How many hours do you want to work a week? _____

- Where do you want to live? In what kind of house
  and neighborhood? _____

- How much money do you want to make per year?_____

- What do you need to be happy? _____
  _____

- Do you want to work by yourself or with people?
  _____

- What industry do you want to be in? _____

SUMMARY

- Many athletes become nostalgic when they stop playing sports because they feel like nothing will ever be as fulfilling as playing sports.

- Live in the present but prepare for the future.

- Derive most of your happiness from the present and future rather than the past.

- It's not too early to start thinking about your professional career plans.

PART II: STRATEGIES AND SYSTEMS

"**It** takes 20 years to build a reputation and five minutes to ruin it. If you think about that, you'll do things differently."

—*Warren Buffet*

CHAPTER 9:
CHARACTER

You cannot be successful and happy in the long run without strong character. This is neither a scientific nor a religious statement but is something I have found to be true through numerous conversations with some of the most successful people in their respective fields. Not everyone who is happy is successful, and not everyone who is successful is happy. However, those who are both always have a strong character. Building character is the most crucial element in your quest for happiness and success. Nothing you learn in this book will be of significance if you don't get this right.

Your character is who you truly are. No one controls it but you. Your reputation, while not unimportant, will change over time and may well be out of your control at times. Your character never is.

Strong character does not just come to people. It is built, earned, and maintained over time. Character reveals itself when you face tough choices, when the bright lights are off, and when the only one to judge you is you.

Nothing builds character like adversity. Whenever you have to leave your comfort zone, you are forced to examine yourself thus building your character. The most successful people I have met do not wait for adversity to force them outside of their comfort zone. They push themselves there every day.

As an athlete, you already apply this when you practice, where the only way to get better is to be uncomfortable, to push yourself outside of your comfort zone. Take weightlifting for example. Any trainer will tell you that growth takes place when you push your muscles beyond a certain point. Only then does your brain realize that your muscle needs to grow stronger or faster to be able to keep up with the new challenges. The same holds true for your character. Only when you stretch your boundaries and challenge yourself will you force yourself to grow as a person.

In order to leave your comfort zone, you first have to realize what it looks like. To examine your own life, start with the following list of typical comfort-zone behaviors:

- Not giving feedback to avoid confrontation
- Lying instead of owning up to mistakes
- Dishonesty or disloyalty during tough times
- Lack of energy and passion, especially when faced with adversity
- Blaming others, the universe, or circumstance for anything
- Doing things only if there is an immediate reward
- Deriving satisfaction from past achievements
- Inaction

It takes willpower and self-discipline to break out of your comfort zone. It also requires that you believe in what you are doing. This belief can be derived from religion, from spirituality, or from rational thought. Most religions emphasize the importance of doing good deeds and exemplifying admirable qualities (compassion, love, humbleness, forgiveness, etc.). Even if you do not believe in anything but rational thought and science, the conclusion is the same: doing right by others will lead to a more fulfilled and happy life. Happiness studies consistently prove the importance of a strong support system of friends and family for a person's happiness. As you will see in later chapters, the way to build a strong support system is to treat people well and to exhibit strong character.

SUMMARY

- Strong character is the foundation for success and happiness.

- Character is built through adversity.

- The most successful people push themselves outside of their comfort zone to experience adversity and therefore grow every day.

"Don't mistake activity for achievement."

—*Coach John Wooden*

CHAPTER 10:
PRODUCTIVE HABITS

Before I do anything, I always ask myself: Is what I'm about to do going to get me better results, make me happier, or help others? These are the only things that matter. Everything else is a waste of time. Results, happiness, and compassion. That's all you need.

THE PARETO PRINCIPLE

In 1906, the Italian economist and philosopher Vilfredo Pareto found that 20 percent of the pea pods in his garden contained 80 percent of the total peas. The curious, scientific mind that he was, he began researching the phenomenon and soon found that 80 percent of the land in Italy was owned by only 20 percent of the people. His findings turned out to be a game-changer for many areas in economics, management, sales, and productivity theory. The Pareto Principle can be observed in many different parts of life. Most businesses derive about 80 percent of their revenue from only 20 percent of their customers, 20 percent of salespeople account for 80 percent of sales, and so on. Applied to your life, the 80/20 rule states that 20 percent of the things you spend your time on lead to about 80 percent of the results you are getting. Realizing this should dramatically change your focus.

As an exercise and future productivity tool, write down 10 things you want to do throughout the day, and list them by how important they are to your success. Then cross off the bottom eight, and focus on doing the top two things incredibly well.

Here is my list:

1.	Finish writing this chapter
2.	Do my taxes
3.	~~Clean my room~~
4.	~~Respond to an email~~
5.	~~Read~~
6.	~~Netflix~~
7.	~~Facebook~~
8.	~~Snapchat~~
9.	~~Go on a date~~
10.	~~Shop online~~

As you can see, I've crossed off the eight items that are unimportant or don't contribute significantly to my results for today. Instead, I'm focusing all my time on the two items that will produce most of my results. Until I finish those first two items, I don't let myself get distracted by any of the other items on the list. When making your list, you should only include items you have full control over. (Don't include tasks that are absolutely essential, as in: don't write down and then cross off "brushing my teeth.")

The 80/20 rule applies to your class work, too. Teachers tend to assign many tasks that have little or no effect on your grade and a few exercises that have a huge impact. For example, I had a professor who based his grade on a class project (35 percent), a final (55 percent), and the homework (10 percent). Although it seems obvious, many students do not approach this situation the right way. They get caught up in daily assignments and forget the big picture.

Here's what I did in this class. I started working on my project right away, went to see my professor during office hours to discuss it, got feedback to make it better, and showed my professor that I was working hard on it. This ensured that he would give me full credit. To prepare for the final, I focused solely on the underlying principles, not the details. I went to every class and took notes on the broad ideas he was teaching, not the anecdotes and background stories. Since the final was cumulative and covered the entire semester, I knew the professor would ask for general principles, not details. I received a 98 on that final. As for the homework, I only turned in the ones that I could do with little time and effort. When I had too much on my plate because of work from other classes, away trips with the team, and so on, the homework in this class was the first thing I skipped. I ended up getting an average of 70 percent on the homework. Since homework accounted for only 10 percent of the total grade, this was enough to secure an A in the class.

Before you get the wrong idea, let's be clear on what this means for you. I'm **not** telling you to skip your homework. Well, not always that is. There is no general rule, except the 80/20 principle, so you will have to use your best judgment. You can't always do everything. It's not possible as a student-athlete; there simply isn't enough time in the day. It is much better to make a conscious decision not to do something than to lose control. I see this happen to student-athletes all the time. Because they are very motivated, they try to do a little bit of everything and end up losing track of their assignments. Usually the result is that they stumble into a test they had forgotten about or forget to turn in an important project. Instead of actively saying no to the 80 percent of tasks that don't matter, they unintentionally mess up the 20 percent of tasks that make all the difference. Tim Ferriss, author of *The 4-Hour Workweek, The 4-Hour Body,* and *The 4-Hour Chef,* said it best:

> *Being overwhelmed is often as unproductive as doing nothing ...*

BATCHING

Simple idea: combining like tasks and finishing things in one sitting will reduce the time you spend on your assignments. The reason is that it takes time to get into the material. Take, for example, the process of writing an essay. If you write it in one sitting all the facts will be fresh, and you'll remember the structure and the details you wanted to include. If you write it over multiple sittings, you'll have to spend time rereading your previous work each time you start. Similarly, if you try to do three different things at once you won't be as effective as if you do three similar things.

This is what most students do during one "productive" hour:

Answer an e-mail, write a little bit of an essay, and read a chapter in their book.

This is what you should do instead:

Write and finish the entire essay you've been assigned.

OR

Answer all your e-mails in one sitting.

OR

Read the assigned book cover to cover.

The idea is to do similar tasks in batches and in one sitting. It will take some discipline to change your routine, but it can save you significant amounts of time. I recommend setting aside certain days for different types of work. I usually did all of my readings on my off day and answered all of my e-mails on Sunday night.

EXERCISE

Identify three times during the week that you can consistently designate for the completion of specific, recurring tasks. For example: do laundry and clean your place every Sunday afternoon.

1. _____

2. _____

3. _____

THE ART OF PROCRASTINATION

The following principle goes against what most, if not all, academic counselors will tell you, and you've probably heard it a million times: Procrastination is bad.

Unfortunately, most high-performing students do it all the time. Beau Levesque, an Academic All-American who graduated with a near-perfect GPA before moving to Spain to play basketball professionally, told me this when I asked him about procrastination:

> *I'm not a good example for procrastination because I would constantly put off assignments. I started to feel like I would perform better on papers if I had an approaching deadline because I wouldn't constantly rethink my thoughts and sentences.*

Without knowing the theory behind it, Beau, like many top students before him, stumbled upon a little known principle called Parkinson's Law and made use of it. The law states that, "work expands so as to fill the time available for its completion." Simply put, the more time you have available, the bigger a given task seems to you. This is problematic for three reasons.

1. Too much time allows your mind to turn a simple assignment into a task that seems impossibly large. This task now hangs over your head for weeks or months, diverting your attention away from more important things. In contrast, a short deadline means you have to get it done, turn it in, and never think about it again.

2. Without urgency you lack focus. It is easy to get distracted by exploring and reconsidering instead of focusing on the essentials.

3. If a deadline is in the far future, it is tempting to do little bits of work every once in a while. This goes against the previously discussed Batching Principle and is a time-waster and productivity killer.

So what is the alternative? You could just procrastinate like everyone else, but, unfortunately, experience shows that traditional procrastination only works for a gifted few. The reason for this is simple: Most classes intensify around the same time during the semester (midterms and finals week, for example). As a result, traditional procrastination means you have to complete everything at once, which leaves you feeling overwhelmed, which is usually when things come crashing down.

The solution is an approach I adopted during my junior year to deal with harder classes. It's called the Fake-Deadline Technique, or FDT for short. It works like this: For any assignment you are given, you limit yourself to the following time frame to complete it: 24 hours for small tasks like homework, 48 hours for larger tasks like group projects or essays, and 72 hours for complex research papers or book reports. Your clock starts when you receive the assignment in class. Right after class you go to the teacher for clarifying questions, then get to work that same day. This is not easy to master, but if done right, it gives you the benefits of procrastination—

namely Parkinson's Law—without any of the problems. If you lack the discipline to put this technique into action, consider involving an academic advisor to hold you accountable.

SOCIAL MEDIA

Social media are productivity black holes. Websites like YouTube, Facebook, and Twitter are designed to keep you on their sites for as long as possible. In fact, the longer you stay, the more advertisements they can show you, and thus the more valuable you become to them. Therefore, they spend a lot of money to make their sites so addicting. Think about the way YouTube presents you with more video options before you have even finished watching the first one. Consider the way Facebook's newsfeed is overflowing with intriguing headlines that prompt you to click and read further. Think about Instagram and how it keeps you scrolling on and on.

Social media can offer great tools and be a source for entertainment, but you have to understand that they are essentially killing your productivity. In the time you took to watch seven cat videos, you could have easily finished your essay. The problem is that most people don't make a conscious decision to use social media. You rarely say: "I'm taking 10 minutes now to check Facebook, post a new picture on Instagram, then it's back to work." Instead you go on there because you're bored, and you start browsing. Next thing you know, 30 minutes have passed, and you still haven't accomplished any of the work you said you were going to do. If you want to remain active on social media but keep your productivity high, here are three key recommendations:

1. Limit the time you spend reading posts and watching videos. Start with videos because they're the most time-consuming. Unless you have nothing else to do, don't even get started on watching YouTube or Vine videos. You can keep posting and tweeting (that usually does not take long). Just don't consume what others share throughout

the day. As a general rule, don't go anywhere near YouTube, Vine, or your newsfeed if you want to be productive. There are two extensions for the Google Chrome browser that will help you with that: Block Site lets you block any website for certain times throughout the day. Newsfeed Eradicator replaces your Facebook Newsfeed with an inspiring quote (every other function on Facebook remains intact).

2. Find a daily routine that involves your social media activity. For example, I usually check my social media sites in the morning to respond to posts and tweets. Throughout the day, I only access social media to post something if I feel like it can't wait, but I never look at anything others have shared. At night, I take some time to browse through the different sites, watch some videos, and read some posts to stay updated on what my friends are up to.

3. Consider uninstalling Snapchat. You'll never get back the time you spend taking that perfect selfie.

PHONE USE

A recent study found that, on average, college males use their phones 6 to 8 hours a day, while college females use their cell phones 8 to 10 hours per day. That means every single day, college students spend more time on their phones than on anything else. If you fall within that range, do yourself a favor and think back on the last year for a second. What do you remember? What good memories come to mind? Of the memories you just recalled, how many involved a tweet, snap, or post? If your answer is "none," maybe it's time to reconsider how you allocate your time.

SUMMARY

- Follow the 80/20 principle: always focus on the 20 percent of tasks that produce 80 percent of the results.

- Batching means completing like tasks together and in one sitting.

- Follow the Fake Deadline Technique: complete every assignment you receive according to a strict, self-assigned deadline.

- Become conscious of your social media habits.

- Consume less meaningless information.

- Reevaluate your time allocation, especially your phone use.

"**Success** is no accident. It is hard work, perseverance, learning, studying, sacrifice, and most of all, love of what you are doing or learning to do."

—*Pelé*

CHAPTER 11:
SCHOOLWORK

The productivity strategies discussed in the previous chapter can transform your academic success if you apply them consistently. In this chapter, you will get a number of additional strategies specific to your time in college.

PARTICIPATION

Try to participate at least twice during every hour you are in class. Be proactive and participate voluntarily. Teachers usually only call on those students who don't participate; by raising your hand voluntarily at least twice per hour, you're positioning yourself among the "exemplary" students who never get called on. This has two very important effects:

1. The teacher will like and remember you.

2. The teacher will never put you on the spot.

Even if you don't know any of the material being discussed in class (say you just got back from a one-week away trip), you can still raise your hand twice an hour just to ask questions. Most teachers don't really differentiate between knowledge participation (answering questions, making useful comments, furthering class discussion) and helpful participation (asking questions, reading some text to the class). To the teacher all that matters is that you're being active and involved. As long as you're perceived as an active, participating student, you will get high participation grades, you won't be called on when you're not ready to answer a questions, and, most importantly, you will have your teacher's sympathy.

Extra Credit

Always do the extra credit. There is no reason why you wouldn't take free points that are just added to your grade. Besides, by not taking advantage of extra credit opportunities you are telling the teacher that you don't care. If you are in between grades at the end of the semester, or need to make a case that the teacher should pass you, having done the extra credit is a strong signal that you did your best. That usually goes a long way.

Teamwork

Teamwork is a huge part of success in any field. I encourage you to collaborate with your classmates as much as possible without breaking the rules. Before a test, work smart and divide the study guide among you and your buddies. Everyone prepares one section of the material; a few days before the exam you each explain your section to the rest of the group. Studies have shown that teaching information to others dramatically increases its retention, so this will be highly effective.

Another way to collaborate involves finding someone who takes great notes. While I do recommend taking notes yourself, oftentimes as an athlete you will miss classes due to traveling. For those days, it is a huge advantage to have a friend who always goes to class and takes beautiful notes. Hint: it's the person who sits in the first row, asks a thousand questions, and stays late after class to chat with the professor about how interesting the political structure of ancient Rome was. That's the person you need to befriend. Be nice, get to know him or her, and be genuine.

That person will save you when finals come around and your notes are nowhere to be found. Ideally, you'll end up making her your study buddy and meeting with her before every test and quiz to get ready. An obvious and incredibly important piece of advice: don't ever use people or make them feel like their worth to you is the sum of things they do for you. Those kinds of relationships might work in the short run, but you will end up regretting ever having treated anyone that way, especially if they looked up to you and were willing to help you.

TIME MANAGEMENT

You have practice, games, trips, school, friends, dates, parties, homework, family, and finals. The first thing you need to do is get a physical calendar or a calendar app. The advantage of a physical calendar that you can carry with you is that you can make it a point to write down every assignment right when the teacher gives it to you. Not only will it keep you from missing anything, it also shows respect to the teacher. So if you do miss something, the teacher will likely be sympathetic since you made such an effort.

Time management is closely linked to productivity. It means applying the 80/20 principle and the FDT to your everyday life. Making time is not enough; you need to learn to maximize it by being productive. The most successful student-athletes I spoke to all had one thing in common: they found routines that worked for them. A routine enables you to do a certain task without having to put any thought into the when and where. This is how Beau Levesque described the routine that enabled him to become an Academic All-American:

"I knew what times of day my mind was the most stimulated and I could work the best in. For example, I finished classes around noon every day and practices were generally at 3:30. If I tried to get any work done between those times, I would be zoning out, exhausted from the mornings classes, dreading practice, and wanting to take a nap. For this reason, after I finished classes, I would eat lunch in the cafeteria, spend a little time with my friends, and then take a nap for almost 2 hours before practice every day. When practice was over, I would eat dinner and then it was time to do homework. Having just finished a workout and eaten, I had no problem sitting down for a few hours and finishing everything I needed to accomplish."

Having a daily and weekly routine to stick to is a much better approach than to do work scattered and at different times every day. You should have a 2-hour time slot set aside every day for studying and doing homework. Choose the time during which you are most productive. Find specific days to deal with any recurring tasks. If something happens every week, like homework, answering e-mails, or reading assignments, you should have a weekly routine that incorporates those things. Remember to always do like tasks in batches and finish assignments in one sitting.

SUMMARY

- Voluntarily participate at least twice for every hour you spend in class.

- Always do the extra credit.

- Work with your classmates and become friends with the people who are smarter than you.

- Get a calendar and keep it updated.

- Find a routine that incorporates 2 hours of focused study time every day.

"I have a calmness and a poise. That comes from starting the day off with meditation."

—*Kobe Bryant*

CHAPTER 12:
LIFE BALANCE

A chieving success as a student-athlete is neither a marathon nor a sprint. The best way to express it with a sports metaphor is to call it *interval training*. For those of you who aren't track athletes, let me explain: interval training simply means alternating bursts of intense activity with intervals of lighter activity. During interval training you sprint for 30 seconds (aka midterms or finals week), then jog lightly for 3 minutes (aka most of the semester).

There is one crucial point to take away from this analogy: Your performance during the sprint critically depends on how well you recover during the jog. If you're not able to catch your breath, bring down your pulse, and remove lactic acid from your muscles, your performance will be worse during the subsequent sprints, and you will eventually break down. Similarly, if you don't relax and prepare when school is easy, you definitely won't excel when it gets tough.

The key is to find a consistent life balance. Think of it as the ideal speed to take during your light jog that will allow you to recover while also moving forward and getting ready for the next sprint. There is no such thing as the one ideal life balance, as it is individual to every person and highly depends on your goals. Put simply, life balance, as it applies to the student-athlete, is your personal combination of academics, athletics, and social life and the time and effort you allocate to each. Your goal is to maximize your total results. Let's consider three different, very extreme types of student-athletes: Mr. NBA-bound, The Party Animal, and The Bookworm.

Mr. NBA-Bound

This highly touted recruit sees college as just another stepping stone to the pros. He's convinced he'll make it, because his supporters have told him so since he was 12 years old. He ignores the possibility of not making it because his mantra is: "Don't listen to the haters." He spends most of his time in the gym, has no interest in learning, and the only professors who like him are the ones who hold season tickets.

+ Upside: If things go well, he'll be a superstar and make lots of money as a pro.

− Downside: If he gets injured, underperforms, isn't as talented as he thinks he is, or decides he wants another career at any point in his life, he is doomed.

The Party Animal

He shows up minutes before the team bus is supposed to leave, wearing sunglasses and reeking of booze. Everyone on campus knows him; he's popular and the life of every party. His Instagram is set to private for a reason. He tested positive for weed twice and was lucky they didn't find evidence of the other drugs he's been taking.

+ Upside: He'll make crazy memories and create a vast network of people who know him.

— Downside: In addition to probably losing his scholarship and ruining his future, he will never reach his full potential as an athlete or a student. The network he has built is not worth as much as he thinks because everyone knows him for what he is: a party animal with little discipline and competence (more on the value of your network later). Worst of all, he is setting himself up for a life of regret and reminiscence because he's investing only in short-term fun and not long-term happiness.

THE BOOKWORM

She started playing sports because her parents thought it would look good on the college application. She's always done what's best for her career, and now she's at a good school. She's a nice kid, but she lacks passion for her sport and for life. She studies because she's always been an overachiever. She's realistic about her athletic career—probably too realistic.

+ Upside: She will do okay as an athlete and very well as a student. She'll end up with a lucrative job offer, and her coaches will have fond memories of her.

— Downside: She might very well wake up one day, 60 years old, and ask herself "Why?" She's never had the answer, and she's missed out on creating memories beyond her professional career. She'll always wonder what could have been, and she'll regret not having lived more fully, focusing on friendships instead of grades and accolades.

These characteristics are exaggerated, but if you're a student-athlete, chances are you've been around people like the ones described above. Don't be one of them! There simply is too much downside for each.

Instead consider another new type of student-athlete: The Scholar Athlete.

THE SCHOLAR-ATHLETE

Coaches, professors, teammates, and opponents alike respect this guy. He shows up on the court or field and in the classroom, and he's confident and social. Professors value his involvement, coaches love his leadership, and teammates respect his work ethic. He has clear goals and grows as a person year after year. He celebrates big wins with his teammates, takes on challenging internships, and spends long nights in the gym—and even longer nights in the library. He'll graduate with honors and, more importantly, with the respect from a large network of friends and supporters who will forever cherish his contributions to the program and the school.

+ Upside: He'll have the time of his life in school. He'll succeed as an athlete, make incredible friendships, and set himself up for a life of happiness.

− Downside: None

Sounds good. Just how do you become that?

It starts by finding your life balance. You've already taken the first steps by establishing a vision for your future and zoning in on your inspiration. The next step is to change your thoughts and actions to fit the life and future you want for yourself.

In college, I used the following principles as the foundation for my life balance. Try them and see what works for you. Everyone is different, so it's important to find your own mix. Remember, it's possible to enjoy your life while excelling as a student and performing as an athlete. These principles will help.

Buddhist State of Mind

Phil Jackson taught it, Michael Jordan and Kobe Bryant embraced it on their way to multiple world titles (further reading: *Sacred Hoops*), and it can change your life. Learning mindfulness was among the hardest things I did in college, but it had the most profound impact. Not only does it allow you to reach a higher level in your sport, it also makes you a better person and student. A study at Northeastern University found that people who practice mindfulness are five times more likely to behave compassionately toward others. If you have ever experienced anxiety or nervousness, you know that they are detrimental to athletic performance. You need to be loose to be at your best. Similarly, if you go into a test or presentation feeling nervous, you won't do as well. Twenty minutes of mindfulness training a day have been found to improve working memory and the ability to sustain attention. Kobe, Phil, and Michael knew what they were doing; mindfulness is well worth the time it takes to learn it.

There are countless ways to master mindfulness; here is a selection of my favorites:

1. **Practice meditation:** Headspace is an amazing iOS and Android app that gives you a different 10-minute guided meditation every day. You can choose different goals like relaxation, focus, or kindness, depending on what area you want to improve.

2. **Look up:** Put your phone away when you are with people. Ask the same from others when you're talking to them. Checking your phone during a conversation is disrespectful and a sign of disinterest. In contrast, not being distracted all the time will increase your presence in the moment and allow you to get more out of life and

improve your relationships. You will become a better listener and radiate attention and full presence at all times. Don't underestimate the effect this has on people.

3. **Get away:** When life gets stressful, finding some peace and quiet can help you stay centered. Going into nature is perfect because you can be alone with your thoughts. Whether it's the mountains, a forest, or a beach, some time away from campus will help you put things in perspective and keep you sane.

4. **Embrace now:** Learn to love every moment as you live it. Free yourself from too much worry about the future by structuring your life and planning ahead. The future only seems worrisome if you're unprepared.

5. **Read up:** LeBron James was able to overcome the pressure of carrying the title hopes of an entire city by simply reading books. If it helped the best player in the world win a title, it can't be such a bad idea. I recommend autobiographies and nonfiction for personal growth and fiction for relaxation, e.g., before going to bed or before high-pressure games.

SEASONAL SOCIAL LIFE

Your life as an athlete consists of different recurring phases throughout the year: preseason, season, off-season, and summer break. I usually partied for two months during the summer break, getting it out of my system, so by the time my season came around, I was happy with Netflix and the occasional night out with the team after a win. Similarly, if you value a wild dating life, do that in the summer, and stay single or have a stable relationship during the season.

SEPARATE SOCIAL CIRCLES

Being part of a sports team is like gaining an additional family. While it is great to be able to make your teammates your best friends, it is important that you build a support system outside of your sport as well. During the season you spend countless days and nights together with your team at airports, hotels, and in the gym. When you do get an off day, it can be helpful to get away and not even think about your sport. When you hear veteran players talk about getting burned out toward the end of the season, it's usually for psychological reasons. Dealing with one thing (your sport) every day is tiring, and you don't want to put yourself in a position where you're so worn out that you lose passion for your sport. The easiest way to prevent that from happening is to:

- Find friends outside of the athletic department.

- Become a member of clubs that have nothing to do with your sport.

- Use your days off to actually spend time away from athletics.

SPECIALIST SUPPORT

Take advantage of the resources that are available to you as a student-athlete. Experts in a variety of fields are there for the sole purpose of helping you. You have access to counselors, tutors, career advisors, and nutritionists, among others; make sure you utilize them. At the beginning of my senior year, I had a personal crisis that lasted for a few months. I was not shooting the ball well, was homesick, and did not feel like my last year in college was going the way I had imagined. After a couple of weeks of dragging myself to practice and class without any enthusiasm, I reached out to the counseling center for help. I started meeting with a counselor once a week. He was able to provide an expert, outside opinion on my problems and helped me through them. He introduced me to meditation and taught me a number of techniques that helped me stay calm during games and boosted my confidence even when my shots were not going in. Six weeks after I started working with him, I was moved into the starting lineup and had my best shooting week at the Great Alaska Shootout, scoring 8 out of 11 three-point shots. Not only did the counseling help me finish the season with a 45 three-point percentage, it also helped me resolve my homesickness. The takeaway here is that asking for help can make all the difference. Don't get caught up in personal pride or think that asking for help means admitting weakness. Most star athletes have mentors and get help with the mental aspects of their game. Counseling in college is free, so take advantage of it. Similarly, tutors are available to help you with your work. Always have your essays checked, and try to go over the material with a tutor before every important test. It comes down to being open about your obstacles and challenges and reaching out when you need help.

SUMMARY

- Find a lifestyle of moderation that you can maintain for four years.

- Explore meditation and other mindfulness techniques.

- Live your social life according to the seasonal phases of your sport.

- Find friends outside of athletics. Spend time away from your sport every once in a while.

- Get help when you need it. Don't be afraid to ask.

"To keep the body in good health is a duty ... otherwise we shall not be able to keep our mind strong and clear."

—*Buddha*

CHAPTER 13: HEALTH AND PERFORMANCE

As a student-athlete, you know your health affects your performance on the field. Chances are that you have always been reasonably healthy and may not have had to learn what it takes to keep your health at its optimum level. Your physical condition does not just affect your athletic performance; it has a large impact on your academic performance. There are two reasons for this:

1. If you are unhealthy, you will not be as happy and balanced. You will, therefore, most likely have a harder time motivating yourself to excel in school.

2. Unhealthy habits directly impact your mental capacity, your level of energy, and your level of focus.

The four topics of this chapter are: nutrition, sleep, recovery from exercise, and drug and alcohol abuse. Each of these factors influences your academic and athletic performance in a variety of ways.

Nutrition

Day to Day

Athletes need to balance their need for a high carbohydrate, high protein diet with their need to keep their fat and overall caloric intake low. Athletes who don't consume enough calories or protein may have trouble maintaining or increasing their strength. Without enough calories, an athlete may also be more susceptible to illness or injury.

So how many calories are enough? According to researchers at the University of Missouri, female athletes should consume 20–23 calories per pound of body weight every day, while male athletes should consume around 23. These calories should be divided as follows:[1]

- 0.5 to 1 gram protein per pound of body weight

- 3 to 5 grams carbohydrates per pound of body weight

- 0.5 grams fat per pound of body weight

Before and After the Game

The following tips will fill you with energy and prevent you from being hungry during the game. You should take the same approach before long tests or other periods that require sustained focus:

- Hydration: drink enough so that your urine is a very light color.

- Avoid caffeine. Drink fruit juice, sports drinks, or water.

- Stop eating 2 to 4 hours before the game.

- If you have the pregame jitters, eat 4 to 6 small meals instead of 3 large meals.

---

1. http://extension.missouri.edu/hes/sportsnutrition/malecalories.htm and http://extension.missouri.edu/hes/sportsnutrition/femalecalories.htm

- Include carbohydrates in your pregame meal. Whole-grain foods like bagels, breads, and crackers are good, as are sports bars or fruit.

- Protein in the pregame meal is important to keep up endurance. Two slices of turkey, a slice of cheese, or a cup of yogurt will do the trick.

Postgame nutrition is just as important. Hard exercise uses the body's energy and fluids, and it breaks down the body's muscles as well. Eating the proper foods and remaining hydrated make all the difference in how quickly an athlete will rebuild muscle and replenish nutrients. Without this, endurance, speed, and accuracy will be affected, as will your mental capacity.

SLEEP

Sleep is critical for the body to repair itself physically as well as for the brain to consolidate memory and release hormones.

Studies have shown that split-second decision making, the kind required during a game, is enhanced in well-rested people. Getting just 2 hours less sleep at night can affect your performance as much as having a 0.05 blood-alcohol level. In addition, a lack of sleep will negatively impact your level of focus and your ability to retain information.

Not only do you need to be asleep for the right number of hours, but your sleep must also be restful. There are many factors that can contribute to a less-than-stellar night's sleep, and, as a student-athlete, you may not have control over all of them. Do your best to control these factors and get an even better night's sleep:

- **Light:** Make sure the room is actually dark. You need melatonin to sleep, and it is only released in the dark.

- **Temperature:** Cool is better than warm. Your body attempts to cool off when you go to bed. If you are in a warm room and cannot cool down, you will not fall asleep as quickly.

- **Noise:** This is hard to control if you are in a dorm. Consider earplugs or a white-noise machine.

- **Comfortable bed:** You can always invest in a mattress topper if you cannot change your actual bed.

- **Beds are for sleeping:** Don't work in bed; work at your desk.

- **Reliable alarm clock:** You will sleep more soundly if you can trust your alarm to wake you.

- **Sleep enough:** Get 8 hours or at least 7½. Any less than that and you risk decreased performance.[2]

RECOVERY FROM EXERCISE

Most athletes are conscientious about preparing for a big game or competition, but it's easy to forget to take care of your body after the event is over. Recovery is critical to prevent overuse syndrome and stress fractures. Putting a little thought and effort into your recovery will allow you to feel better over the next few days and will help determine how well you do at the next game.

It is important to eat and drink after a workout or a game. The sooner you replenish your stores of energy and fluids, the faster your recovery will be. Within 20 to 30 minutes of your workout, you should eat about 0.5 grams of carbohydrates per pound of body weight. Within 2 hours, you should eat an additional 0.5 grams of carbohydrates per pound of body weight. Make sure to rehydrate as well. The carbohydrates and electrolytes in sports drinks will help your body both rehydrate and refuel.[3]

You may be tempted to crash on the couch after a big game, but don't. You need to keep your blood circulating well to get rid of the lactic acid

---

2. http://www.webmd.com/sleep-disorders/features/sleep-like-an-olympian
3. http://www.washingtonpost.com/wp-dyn/content/article/2010/11/09/AR2010110903278.html

produced by exercise, and you will also want to keep your muscles as limber as possible.

Gentle exercise, from a slow cool-down run to yoga to a walk or a slow bike ride, will help your recovery. Of course, you should stretch as much as possible, too, even several hours after your game. The only bad thing you can do during a recovery period is to just sit.

After strenuous exercise, nothing feels better than a hot shower or whirlpool. Athletes have been doing this for years. Unfortunately, the opposite may be what is best for your recovery. Cold water immersion, or ice baths, will reduce the swelling in overworked legs by constricting the blood vessels and decreasing metabolic activity. This reduces swelling and tissue breakdown.

DRUG AND ALCOHOL ABUSE

Drug Abuse

It's not easy to avoid drugs and alcohol in college, but, as an athlete, it is critical for your performance. In this section, we speak of drugs in two ways, first as performance-enhancing drugs and second as recreational drugs. For your long-term health, you should avoid both.

Performance-Enhancing Drugs

Our nation reveres its winners and forgets its losers. Winning is the only important part of the game, and only winning brings popularity, fame, scholarships, and status. With so much on the line, it is not surprising that athletes today look for any advantage, no matter how small.[4]

There are different types of performance-enhancing drugs, including androstenedione, creatine, and ephedra alkaloids. All three are available over the counter and are no longer controlled by the FDA. Without

---

4. http://www.addictionhope.com/prescription-drugs/pressure-on-athletes-competitiveness-and-addiction

oversight, these supplements vary in their purity and efficacy, and any marketing claims—including "safe" and "natural"—can be made without legal repercussions.

Creatine is a fine white powder. Most people need about 2 grams of creatine in their diet every day. It is important because it is used in the production of ATP, the chemical that powers the cells. Taking additional creatine will, in theory, increase the amount of energy athletes have at their command.

If only it were that simple. The adverse effects of creatine include:

- Water retention
- Weight gain above and beyond water retention
- Muscle damage from overuse
- Kidney dysfunction

The long-term effects have not yet been studied in detail but the possibility of kidney damage is too high a price to pay.

Androstenedione and its derivatives convert to testosterone in the liver. This added testosterone allows both male and female athletes to build more muscle over a shorter period of time, giving them a competitive edge. New studies indicate that these drugs raise levels of both testosterone and estrogen in the blood.

Side effects include:

- Irreversible gynecomastia, growth of breasts in men
- Closure of bone-growth plates
- Acne
- Hair loss
- Testicular atrophy
- Changes in personality
- Aggression or "roid rage"

These drugs have been banned by several sports governing bodies, including the IOC, NCAA, and NFL.

Recreational Drug Abuse

An athletic career is stressful, and so is the path to get there. As a student-athlete you might feel increased pressure to perform on the field, in the classroom, and even in social situations.

The rush of competition and winning can become addictive. This sense of competition encourages high standards for the student, set by a combination of coaches, teammates, parents, teachers, fans, and the student. With seemingly everyone expecting something from the student, he or she is bound to fail occasionally.

Student-athletes may worry about letting all these people down, and they may think that the loss of a game or a season is the same as becoming a complete failure in all aspect of their lives.

This incredible stress can lead student-athletes to turn to drugs for an escape. Common student addictions include prescription painkillers like morphine, methadone, Vicodin, and Percocet. Student-athletes have also been known to abuse Adderall, Ritalin, and cocaine.[5]

Athletes often first use painkillers for a legitimate injury. The problem is that those painkillers can be highly addictive. They depress the central nervous system, much like alcohol, which results in short-term feelings of well-being and euphoria. This results in an increased sense of self-esteem, relieving the athlete of the performance-related pressures inherent in his life.

As with many drugs, the longer they are taken, the higher tolerance the athlete develops and addiction is not far behind.

Athletes turn to stimulants to boost their performance as well. The most common of these are Adderall, Ritalin, and cocaine. These drugs help the athlete stay alert, maintain focus, and reduce fatigue. However, they can also cause athletes to have an enhanced sense of aggressiveness on the field.

---

5. http://www.nationwidechildrens.org/abuse-of-drugs-to-enhance-sports-performance-winning-at-any-cost

These drugs provide a quick burst of energy and concentration. As with all drugs, the effects wear off. The effects of cocaine last for about 30 minutes, while the prescription stimulants last for 6 hours.

As with prescription pain killers, tolerance levels increase and the athlete becomes addicted. Addicted athletes will crave the drug and feel as though they cannot perform without it.

Alcohol Use and Abuse

The average college student drinks somewhere around 34 gallons of alcohol every year. This can be as much as 20 percent of the student's caloric intake. While many people think drinking alcohol in college is part of the experience, it does not have to be, particularly for student-athletes. Alcohol and athletics do not mix well. Side effects of drinking include dehydration, lowered testosterone levels, impaired reaction time, additional fat storage, and depression. If you feel you must drink, save it for the off season.

Alcohol is a diuretic, which means that it pulls water out of your body. Even if you had a couple of beers the night before the game and are no longer under the influence, your body is still dehydrated. When dehydrated, you may suffer from cramps and muscle pulls and strains. In extreme cases, when coupled with intense practices or games, dehydration will lead to brain impairment and death. Muscle loss and decreased appetite lead to muscle wasting or the loss of muscle mass. You work so hard to put strong muscle on, why throw it away on alcohol?

Binge drinking, defined as 5 drinks for men or 4 drinks for women in any 2-hour period, decreases the level of testosterone in the blood. This leads to loss of lean muscle mass, slower muscle recovery time, and a decrease in athletic performance.[6] Male athletes may see breast enlargement, testicular shrinkage, and decreased sperm count. Female athletes may show an increase in levels of estradiol, which may increase the risk of breast cancer.

---

6. http://www.nmnathletics.com/attachments1/507.htm?DB_OEM_ID=5800

You know your reaction time and mental acuity is hampered when you are drinking alcohol, but did you know it can be impaired up to several days later? Not only will your performance be diminished, but your risk of injury is higher.

Alcohol is not a low-calorie drink. It has 7 calories per gram, second only to fat, which has 9 calories per gram. Alcohol turns to sugar in the digestive system, which is then stored as fat. In addition, alcohol destroys the amino acids from which proteins are formed and stores them as fat. Not only does alcohol increase body fat, it also decreases lean muscle.

Binge drinking can lead to fatty liver, fibrosis, cirrhosis, and gout. Alcohol overstimulates the stomach lining cells to create more acid. When this happens, micronutrients are not absorbed properly, and this leads to electrolyte imbalances.

Although you may feel happy while you are drinking, alcohol depresses the central nervous system. Alcohol impairs judgment, which can lead to fights, auto accidents, homicides, and suicides.

Alcohol has numerous side effects, and it plays a part in preventing athletes from reaching peak fitness. If more than one player on a team has consumed alcohol in the days before a game, that entire game can be compromised.

Being a college athlete is a difficult job. Please don't make it harder on yourself by not taking good care of your body and your mind.

SUMMARY

- Taking care of your body will help your mind perform better as well.

- Keeping in mind your nutrition and sleep needs and your recovery times is essential to your success.

- Treat exams like games: get enough sleep and eat high-nutrient foods beforehand.

- Drugs are not worth the damage to your body and the risk to your career.

- If you must drink alcohol, do it during the off-season.

"We must take care of our families wherever we find them."

—*Elizabeth Gilbert*

CHAPTER 14:
SUPPORT SYSTEM

YOUR FAMILY

I left Germany when I was 17 for one year and then again when I was 21, that time for good. I lived in three different places over the course of five years, and, every time, I had to find new friends and start my life from scratch. All of my family was back in Germany, so I was completely alone starting out. Add to that the 9-hour time difference and subsequent difficulty of staying in touch, and you can imagine how lonely I was at times. What saved me was the fact that I had teammates and coaches. At Cuesta, my team consisted of 10 international athletes and 2 Americans. I lived with people in the same situation that I was in, and they became my family. Homesickness can be really hard, especially if you are as close to your family as I am. There are a number of effective ways of dealing with homesickness:

- **Mindset:** Do not dwell on the fact that things are happening at home without you around. Your family and friends might still be there living their old lives, including some of the things you love doing, but you have an opportunity to do something great. Don't let your homesickness get in the way.

- **Your new family:** Try to socialize a lot in the beginning to find the people that you want to get to know better and spend time with. Don't stay glued to your room; go out, meet people, and make things happen.

- **Support system:** Most schools offer great support systems in the form of counseling and/or health centers. Take advantage of those. Your mind, just like your body, needs nurturing. You will have tough times; that's part of the experience. However, if you feel depressed, lonely, or homesick for weeks, seek out help on campus.

- **Stay busy:** This is obvious. The best medicine for homesickness is creating memories, working hard in your sport, and spending time with friends.

No-Nonsense Networking

> *You are the average of the 5 people you spend the most time with.*
>
> ~Jim Rohn

The network you build while in school will accelerate your career later on—if it is built the right way, with the right people. There are two types of networks you will form:

1. Your inner circle (includes teammates and friends)

2. Your extended network

Your *inner circle* is crucial. You cannot pick your teammates, so that part is outside of your influence. However, you do decide with whom you spend time away from your team. Don't underestimate the effect this will have on your life. Stay away from people with negative, narrow-minded, or limited views. Instead, surround yourself with people who challenge you, inspire you, and make you better. If the people around you aren't doing much, it's easy to be complacent, too. If your best friends dream big and work hard, they will inspire you to become your best self as well.

While your inner circle is crucial in shaping the person you become, your *extended network* will give you the access and connections to get a foot in the door whenever you need it, wherever you need it. These factors determine the value of your extended network:

- The people who are in it

- What those people think of you

The reach of your network (the number of people) matters, but that's not nearly as important as *who* those people are. Ideally, you should build a network of influence, access, and knowledge. Most importantly, the people in your extended network have to have potential. It's great if they can help you right now, but what about in ten years? Some of the people at your school will be CEOs, politicians, and investors in the future. Make sure they'll remember who you are!

Having a large network of influential people is worth little to nothing if those people don't value and respect you. It's not enough to be liked. People will only open doors for you (make introductions, recommend you, invest in you, and so on) if they believe in your competence and abilities. The reason is simple: anyone who recommends you, or vouches for you, puts their reputation on the line if you don't deliver or perform. Your performance always reflects on those who associate with you. That means if you are known as a competent, loyal, well-connected person, everyone is going to want to help you because it makes them look good. Also, people tend to do things out of self-interest, so if they believe in your ability to help them later on, they are more likely to help you now. A strong network is always built on mutual respect for what the other person brings to the table.

So how do you make sure your network knows your value and will pick up the phone, eager to help you when the time comes?

- **Be memorable:** I learned this from our former graduate assistant Ricky, who's Italian. Wherever he went, Ricky made it a point to be the most memorable person in the room. His straightforwardness paired with his hilarious Italian accent ensured that anyone who talked to him would remember him even months later. Going anywhere in LA with him is like attending a big reunion because, no matter the place, people know Ricky the Italian.

- **Be valuable:** Make sure people perceive you as a person with high value. Instead of constantly asking others to make decisions and help you, try offering up solutions and valuable insights. If you can connect people for their mutual benefit, always do it. The most influential people I have met constantly look to connect the people in their network with each other.

- **Be helpful:** If you help others constantly without asking for anything in return, those favors will form a powerful network. Don't get in the habit of thinking "What can that person do for me?" If you can help, don't think about it, just do it. Some of the best opportunities I have had have come completely unexpectedly from people I helped many years ago and whom I never expected to even see again.

- **Be present:** To get to know people, you have to be around them. You will probably never find a better place to network than your university campus. Joining clubs and student organizations, going to on-campus events, and taking part in student activities are essential to building your network.

- **Be observant:** When I went to Admit Weekend at Stanford, I got to meet over 100 of my future classmates. One of them was a German student who had worked at Google for six years before deciding to go to business school. While I was overwhelmed with the number of names, faces, and stories, he was able to remember the name of every single person at the event in the two days we were there. Blown away by his memory, I asked him for his secret. He replied:

> *Most people lack intent. They focus on things like their appearance, handshake, or what they should say; their thoughts are somewhere else entirely. I focus on one thing only: who is this person I'm meeting right now.*

He repeated names in conversation, asked interesting questions, and listened very actively. This, along with strong visual-memory techniques (more later in the memory chapter), allowed him to stand out and, in only two days, build a network of over 100 future business leaders.

- **Be bold:** This goes along with being memorable. You can't be afraid to talk to people. If you're shy, start working on it. Listing all the different strategies for overcoming shyness would go beyond the scope of this book. Just one tip: if you are shy, set rules for yourself that force you to overcome your shyness on a daily basis. Being bold is especially important when you have the chance to connect with an influential person—an athletic booster who owns a company or a speaker at an on-campus event. Go up and introduce yourself at some point. Ask for their e-mail address or business card in case you ever need advice. It doesn't matter if you're not sure you'll ever use it. Collect it anyway; one day you'll be thankful you did.

TURNING PROFESSORS INTO MENTORS

If I had a penny for every time a teammate blamed a bad grade on personal dislike by a professor—well, I'd be rich. The thing is, most of the time my teammates were right: the professor actually did not like them. But can you really blame the professor?

Professors are human, they make mistakes, and they like some people and dislike others—just like we all do. All too often, it appears random and unfair and sometimes it is. However, most professors just dislike the students that don't show them respect. Professors are experts in their field. They've spent years acquiring the knowledge to teach at the university level. So they take offense to people who do not value their wisdom and intellect. If you're usually late, sleep through class, and don't show any interest, chances are your professors won't show you much love.

Your professor controls your grades the same way your coach controls your playing time. Your performance matters, but they can always bench you for any reason. Getting your professors on your side will not only help your grades, it will also provide you with influential supporters for your career later on. During my senior year, I was contacted multiple times by large companies interested in hiring me—because my professors had referred me to their friends in the business world.

Making your professor like you does not take much effort or time. The key is to be respectful and not to look down on them, especially if you are a star on campus because of your sport. You will have to break the perception that athletes are dumb and arrogant, so start by introducing yourself to your professor after the first class period. Be kind, and show that you are trying. Sit somewhere near the front, especially in large classes, and participate whenever you can. Most importantly, let your professors in. They generally want to help, but they need a good reason. In my junior year, I had my hardest class, Applied Econometrics, at 8 a.m. Our workouts from 5 to 7:30 a.m. left me drained and tired, and I often fell asleep during class. After the second time, I went up to the professor after class and told him that my falling asleep was not a sign of disinterest but rather of fatigue from the hard practices. He told me that he appreciated my openness. After that, he always made jokes about my falling asleep whenever I saw him outside of class. When I applied to grad schools, he wrote my letter of reference, which played a key role in getting into Stanford.

MENTORS

I stumbled across my mentor at a Pepperdine Entrepreneur Club meeting. Her name was Hope, which I have always found very fitting. She encouraged me to start my first company, met with me almost every month, and provided me with support and guidance whenever I felt lost. When I had a big decision to make, or just wanted to talk something through, I could count on her advice and honest opinion.

A mentor can accelerate your personal growth by challenging you, giving you advice based on their experiences, and opening up doors with their connections. There are certain qualities your mentor should possess. Some of them are:

- **Experience:** Your mentor needs to be able to give you advice based on what they have been through.
- **Competence:** Your mentor should know what they are talking about, especially in the industry you want to work in.
- **Character:** Your mentor has to have the strong character you want to develop yourself.
- **Role model:** You should try to find a mentor who can be a role model for you and who is living the life you want for yourself.

EXERCISE

Who do you consider a mentor? What qualities does he or she possess? Is there anyone you know who can help you explore career opportunities outside of your sport? If so, write them an e-mail right now.

_____

_____

_____

_____

_____

_____

_____

_____

Finding a mentor can be challenging. It's not something I recommend you do actively. Don't start e-mailing random people asking them to be your mentor. I never spoke to my mentor Hope about mentorship. I simply got to know her and wasn't afraid to ask her for advice. The key is to put yourself in a position where you can meet interesting people in leadership positions. On-campus speaker events, conferences, networking functions, and student clubs are great ways to get to know potential mentors. Once you connect with someone, make an effort to get to know him or her and show that you are eager to learn from them. Remember that, at the end of the day, everyone you meet, no matter how successful they are, is just another human being with interests, struggles, and opinions. So don't be afraid to connect with them on a personal level rather than a professional one. If you make an effort and ask for advice, most people are very willing to help.

SUMMARY

- Surround yourself with people who challenge you, inspire you, and make you better.

- Actively build your network. Make sure people know your value.

- Help others, connect people in your network, and create value for people whenever you can.

- Turn your professors into mentors and supporters by showing respect and letting them be part of your life.

- Be bold, be memorable, and be helpful.

- Find at least one mentor in the industry you plan to work in after your athletic career.

"Perception is reality."

—*Unknown*

CHAPTER 15:
PERSONAL BRANDING

I t's no secret that getting a good job today is tougher than it used to be. It sounds like a cliché, but you're now competing with people from all over the world for jobs. You're competing with the work ethic of a student from China who is used to spending 14+ hours a day in school. You're up against the creativity of a graphic designer in India who taught herself how to use all of the Adobe® products and has been creating designs since age 12. You're trying to beat out a young man from Europe who's fluent in five languages. I'm not exaggerating; that's the reality. Just as it is in most sports, the higher up you get, the stiffer and more international the competition becomes.

On top of significant international competition, your own classmates have an advantage over you as well: they spent their summers interning and gathering work experience while you were busy perfecting your jump shot/tackle/pitch.

What are you supposed to do?

You could try to beat your competition at their own game: outwork the student from China, outdesign the woman from India, outspeak the boy from Europe. It's possible, just not given your time constraints and commitments as an athlete. You could cut back on the time you spend on your sport and work/intern instead. Is this really an option? Wouldn't you risk living the rest of your life wondering how good you could have been had you given everything to your sport?

That leaves you with just one option: turn your "weakness" into a strength. Make the fact that you've been an athlete for most of your life your biggest asset. If phrased correctly, it is fairly easy to convey the significant advantages of the training you have received as an athlete. You're more disciplined, have more endurance, are used to performing under pressure and on little sleep, are capable of working on a team, and are not afraid to lead.

There are still people who believe athletes are stupid and incapable of doing anything other than their sport. That is a perception you have to not only overcome but completely reverse. That's why personal branding needs to be at the center of your career planning. It's the only way to actively break the stereotype.

Personal branding includes everything that may affect the perception people have of you and what you stand for. If done right, people in your network (and eventually those outside of it) will start to associate your name with certain positive qualities. Make sure you become known as loyal, trustworthy, influential, and capable. Once your reputation is tarnished, it can take a long time to fix. This does not mean you should try to please everyone. There will always be people who disagree with you or envy your achievements. The key is to live by the principles of results, happiness, and compassion and to align the perception people have of you with the character you display. Unfortunately, people's perception will not always reflect the reality of your character. I had a friend who was a great all-around guy, but his hygiene was subpar, and so people's perception of him (smelly, doesn't take care of himself) did not at all reflect his great character (loyal, reliable, smart). Personal branding is the best way to make sure that doesn't happen to you. The following are my rules for building a strong personal brand.

RULE #1: BECOME AN EXPERT

The most powerful way to create a personal brand that has value in the business world is to become an expert. Focus on one specific industry you want to work in after your athletic career. Becoming an expert takes time, as you have to build competence first. Status is meaningless without substance. Don't use personal branding to present yourself as something you're not. Make sure you actually know the industry well, then aggressively brand yourself by sharing what you know and connecting with industry leaders.

Utilize Twitter and LinkedIn to share articles, blog posts, and videos relevant to your industry. Your Twitter feed should feel relevant to anyone from your industry looking you up. Ideally, you should start your own blog on a subject related to your industry.

Join at least one club on campus that relates to your industry. I joined the Entrepreneur Club in my junior year and benefited in a number of ways. I made some great connections and, as I noted in the last chapter, met a mentor I still turn to for advice. I also took part in a business-pitch competition that gave me very practical training in what raising money for my company would be like and introduced me to numerous investors.

Reach out to experts in the field and seek advice. The best way to get in touch is in person. Schools often bring in speakers for various events. Go to as many industry-related events as you can. Research the speaker(s) beforehand and have at least two points from their bio ready to compliment them on or ask them about. After they finish speaking, go up, introduce yourself, and ask specific questions that show them that you are familiar with their work. Then get a business card/phone number/e-mail address!

Another way to gain valuable connections in your industry is to utilize LinkedIn. Reach out to a few people in your extended network every month. Make sure to research their background and to include in your message a specific question about their work or something they did that you find interesting.

Rule #2: Look Sharp

Dress as if you belong: This will be the hardest thing for you. I know, because it was for me. I grew up wearing sweats, basketball shorts, and sneakers. No suit or button-down will ever be as comfortable. Understand, however, that first impressions matter and that you have to overcome the stereotype "student-athlete" in order to build a successful personal brand and gain respect in the business world. I recommend going to any function or event looking sharp: dark jeans or pants, button-down shirt, and dress shoes for guys; professional-looking dress or a dark skirt or pants with a dark jacket and light cotton shirt or blouse for gals, as well as quality leather shoes. Select colors in dark, classy shades such as black, brown, navy blue, or grey. Whenever you have a chance of encountering someone who matters (boosters, speakers, professors, business recruiters), make sure you look like you belong. This isn't about changing who you are; it's about showing that you are comfortable in the business world. Don't fight the invisible man; the only one you're punishing with that is yourself. I don't know who made the dress code for the business world, and I would much rather go in sweats, too. But trust me, people have a different kind of respect for successful professional men and women than for athletes.

Smell good: Don't be the person who wears the same t-shirt three days in a row or who has bad breath. You're an adult now, so take care of yourself. Brush your teeth at least twice a day, shower at least once a day and after every workout, use deodorant and some cologne or perfume. For guys the rule of thumb is to shave every three days.

If you must stand out, stand out looking fresh: A James Harden beard? A brightly colored dress à la Serena Williams? A Russel Westbrook shirt or glasses? You can make whatever fashion statement you want, just as long as you look sharp. If a CEO saw you today, would he or she still hire you tomorrow?

Rule #3: Build an Online Presence

This is not optional anymore. You need to control your online presence and use it to your advantage. It should enhance your brand and allow you to increase your network.

Twitter

Tweet and build followers. That's actually really positive and can help you a lot later on, especially if you ever start your own business. Just make sure whatever you say is smart. Try to provide value from time to time. Post links to interesting videos or articles that relate either to your sport or to the professional industry you wish to work in after your athletic career. Again, it's all about making sure you're not just another athlete.

LinkedIn

Start building your profile immediately. Make sure the intro text is well written and outlines your experience as an athlete and your aspirations as a professional. Your profile photo should have a professional look and feel. Again, you want to look like you belong. Then, start adding everyone you know and everyone you want to know. Reach out to business leaders in your extended network every once in a while, compliment them on their latest article or blog post, and let them know you're excited to connect with them.

Your Personal Website

Use GoDaddy or any other domain reseller to purchase a website with your first and last name: www.FirstNameLastName.com. If that domain is taken, get the .net or .info domain. When you become a senior, set up your website and update it regularly. Over time, your website will start ranking with Google, and every time someone looks up your name, your website will show up first. That's important because it allows you to control the information people find about you first.

To build your website, use any of these services:

- **www.strikingly.com**—Customize and publish a site without coding knowledge.

- **www.wordpress.com**—Wordpress is the most-used content management system on the planet. By using a template (cost ranges $0–$60; the X Theme template is my favorite), you can build a great-looking site with very few coding skills.

- **www.godaddy.com**—Use GoDaddy.com for buying domains and hosting the website. Their customer service is unmatched, and their prices are pretty good.

SUMMARY

- Aggressively brand your experience as an athlete to turn a disadvantage into a selling point.

- Become an expert in the field you are most interested in and make sure you are perceived as such.

- Always look like you belong.

- Build an online presence to support your career.

PART III: SKILLS AND TOOLS

"Get out. I need to go to my mind palace."

—*Sherlock Holmes*

CHAPTER 16:
MEMORY MASTERY

Remember the person in class who never seemed to study but always got full points on every test? I was that person, and this chapter contains every strategy and technique I used to make learning simple. Most of the techniques I use are not my own inventions. I borrowed them from memory world champions who use them to recall over 22,000 random numbers in order or to remember 200 faces with names in less than 5 minutes. What you have in front of you is a collection of the best approaches to memorization, supplemented with my own strategies and simplified into actionable strategies.

First, you need to understand roughly how information is processed and stored. Your brain is made up of cells called neurons that process and store information. These neurons use signals, called synapses, to transmit information and connect to one another. I won't bore you with the details, but the key takeaway here is this: the more connections any one neuron has to others, the less likely it is to fade away. This is the reason why some childhood memories are impossible to get rid of. You've built so many connections around it (e.g., smell, touch, relating stories, etc.) that your brain has determined that this piece of information is indispensable. As a result your brain is providing the necessary maintenance for the neurons in question to keep the information alive.

Now, if you want to retain new information, the key is to build as many connections around it as possible. This is the foundation for all the following tips and tricks I will give you. One more thing you should know before we dive in is that images and visuals are by far the most effective way to learn. The reason for this is evolution. During simpler times, visual memorization was essential to survival. Knowing what a dangerous animal or a poisonous mushroom looked like often meant the difference between life and death. As a result, evolution has equipped us with a strong ability to visually memorize, which is a skill we will make extensive use of in this chapter. In addition, images contain much more information and detail than spoken or written words. One of the important tools we will learn in this chapter, therefore, will be to translate anything we read or hear into images we can easily remember.

The ideal process of learning includes any number of the following five strategies. The more you use any piece of information, the more likely it is that you'll remember it.

1. Engage with the information.

2. Repeat and practice.

3. Relate to existing knowledge.

4. Use visuals.

5. Organize and support.

ENGAGE

Good memory starts before you even receive the information. Before you read or hear presumably important information, make up assumptions about what you expect and hope to learn. Ask yourself questions that you expect a text to answer before reading it. Think about what you want a speaker to talk about given the headline of his or her presentation. While receiving the information, constantly go back to the questions you started out with. Are they being answered? Are your expectations being met? If not, why? This takes only about 30 seconds and leads you to engage with the presented material more deeply.

Why does this approach work? Curiosity has been found to significantly increase memory. If you're not naturally curious about a subject, you have to trick your brain into thinking about information the same way it would if you were actually curious about it.

REPEAT AND PRACTICE

Next, make sure to repeat and practice the information as often as possible and in different settings. Write it down, talk about it, and teach it to others. Explaining the material to others ensures that you actually know the cause-and-effect relationships and ingrains the information in a much more substantial way by connecting it to a new, more memorable setting (talking to people is more memorable than the page of some history book).

RELATE TO EXISTING KNOWLEDGE

The goal is to create many connections between the neurons. If you have to remember a new name, connect it to someone you know who has the same name and imagine those two people meeting each other. If you have to remember a complicated word, consider splitting it up into shorter words that you can connect to other sounds or words in a logical way that allows you to retrieve it later.

Use Visuals

This is hands-down the most effective way to memorize anything. Academic All-American Beau Levesque summarized his studying strategy as follows:

> *My studying technique for exams was always kind of weird. For tests with study guides or notes that I knew were going to be on the exam, I would hand-write my study guide, never on more than one page front and back. I would use a ton of different colors and sizes of writing. Some would be slanted, and others would be in different shaped boxes so that every section of the notes looked different. I would read this page front and back countless times until I had it committed to memory. Then, when I read the test, I would think about where on the page that section was, and I could always remember it.*

The reason why this approach works so well is that Beau gave his brain visual clues to supplement the plain information. His brain linked different information to different colors, shapes, and places on the page, which made it easier for him to remember.

There are other even more effective ways to use visuals. Beau's strategy was limited to colors and shapes. If you want to take it one step further, try drawing little images for as many informational pieces as possible. Columbus began his journey to the New World in 1492? Draw a little blue ship with the red number 1492 on it. Then close your eyes, and imagine an actual ship as vividly as possible, with as much detail as you can add. How big is the ship? What color is the sail? What does the number 1492 look like on the sail?

Once you've mastered this visual technique, you can turn any piece of information into an image, add some detail, store it, and then retrieve it with all its detail when you need it.

Not all images are created equal. Some will escape your brain more quickly than others. These rules will help you choose the right images to remember:

1. **Make it inappropriate:** The more outrageous, sexual, or violent an image, the easier it is to remember. If it makes you uncomfortable, chances are you won't forget it.

2. **Logic trumps creativity:** If the connection is logical, you will always be able to recall it; if it's creative, you might not be able to.

3. **Add detail:** More detailed images are easier to remember. You can store numerous informational pieces within one image. For example a mental image of an astronaut might include his nametag, which reads Neil Armstrong, the American flag on his arm, and the number 1969 tattooed on his face (remember: make it outrageous, but logical!). One simple image storing three critical facts.

4. **Make it personal:** Try connecting the image to something you know very well, like a childhood memory.

The following is an example from a history class I once took. For a test, I had to memorize the names Socrates, Plato, and Aristotle, the order in which they lived, and their contributions to philosophy.

First I took the first letters of each of their names and formed the word SPA, which also gave me the order in which they lived: Socrates first, then Plato, then Aristotle. Then I imagined an actual SPA. In fact, I imagined a SPA in Malibu that I used to go to and the following scene taking place: Socrates reading a big law book (an image that symbolizes one of his most significant contributions, the dialectic method), Plato sitting at his feet (showing that he was Socrates' student) holding a red heart in one hand

and a weirdly shaped vase in the other. This reminded me of his philosophical writings about platonic love and the theory of form. Finally, I pictured Aristotle holding a Rubik's Cube. I associated this with logic, to remind me that his contributions were mostly in the field of logic.

This story might not mean much to you, but it ensures that I will never forget what each of these 3 philosophers contributed to philosophy and who came first.

Organize and Support

Organizing information makes it easier for the brain to process and store it. The following techniques will help you structure information the right way:

- **Outlines:** When studying for a test, start by gathering all the information that you may need. Then break it up into sections, either by topics, chapters, or in the order in which you learned about it in class. Boil the information down to the absolute essentials. Don't write down things you already know. Instead focus on unknown facts, critical words, and important dates. Instead of "In 313 A.D., Constantine issued the Edict of Milan, which legalized Christianity," write "313 ➔ Constantine ➔ Edict of Milan ➔ Christianity." Next, write this condensed information on a single sheet of paper. Use different colors for different sections, make little drawings, and structure the paper in a way that logically reflects the information. Family trees, graphs, pyramids, charts, and lists are great visual elements that will make your study sheet more memorable.

- **Name mnemonics:** Use the first letters of words or names you have to remember. If there is a list of ten words, take the first letter of each word and form a memorable word out of them to be able to recall it later.

- **Note cards:** Note cards are a good way to supplement your studying. Always write your outline before making the note cards, and make sure the cards have exactly the same information and wording as the outline. If they differ, you'll end up studying wrong information.

- **The Marker Strategy:** This technique is particularly effective when you have to read long texts and remember as much detail as possible. A marker is a visual image you create while you are reading. Each marker contains as many relevant details as possible. Every paragraph should have two to four markers, and every marker should have three to five details. The example with Socrates, Plato, and Aristotle sitting in a SPA holding different objects would be one marker.

- **The Memory Palace:** In order to use this technique you have to prepare by "building" your memory palace. Choose a place you are very familiar with. Your childhood home is a good example. It can be a house, an apartment, or any other building that you know inside and out. Start by closing your eyes and imagining walking through your chosen place. Recall as many details as possible. What furniture is in there? Does it have a kitchen? What are the wall colors? How many rooms? Who lives in each room? Next, you have to choose a route through the place and remember it. It should have at least 50 steps. For example, my route starts when I open the door to my childhood home. It's an old wooden door with two locks. I can see it in front of me clearly. The second step of my route is the shoe rack. The third step is stepping into the hallway and yelling "hello" to my mom. I picture the hallways, with two pictures on the wall. The fourth step is a mirror at the end of the hallway. And so on. You get the point. Imagining all of these steps and making it a very familiar route will take some time, but once you know it, you never have to come up with a new one again. This route will allow you to store as many pieces of information as you have steps in your route. Let's use the first four steps of my route from the previous example to store four historic events from World War II in the right order:

* On my old wooden door there is a piece of paper nailed to it that has the year 1933 and the name Hitler written on it. I step inside and take off my shoes. There are three shoes on the top shelf and eight on the second, and there are pieces of glass all over the shoe rack. This helps me memorize the year 1938 in which the Nazis attacked Jewish stores, smashing in windows. I step in the hallway, and there are pearls on the ground everywhere and the number 41 is painted in red and white on the wall. This helps me recall Pearl Harbor and the year Japan attacked the United States. I walk down the hallway and see myself in the mirror. I have the number 1945 tattooed on my forehead and I'm holding a white flag. The image helps me recall the year in which Germany was finally defeated.

* These kinds of images are much harder to forget than simple names and data points. Once you have a memory palace that you're familiar with, it's very easy. Any kind of data can be stored with just a little creativity. Moving along the familiar route will help you recall events, names, and places in the right order.

It sounds crazy—and that's exactly why it is so effective. You have a choice: either do what you've always done and get the same mediocre results everyone else is getting, or do something uncommon and get exceptional results. Trust me, the look on your professor's face when you recite 100 events in order will be priceless.

The Major Memory System

Okay, you are serious about improving your academic performance. You get that it is important for you to build a future outside your sport. You've implemented all the basic methods in this book, but you're not satisfied. You want to be perfect. This section is for you.

Ever wondered how national memory champions can memorize over 22,000 numbers in order? I used to think they were geniuses, gifted in a way I could not even begin to understand. I often struggled to memorize even the most basic things, like my friends' phone numbers, so I thought people who could memorize 100 times that had to be gifted in some way that I was not.

Turns out I was wrong. Memory masters do not have genius capabilities. They've just trained themselves to use certain techniques really well, allowing them to store numbers much more effectively than the average person. In this section, I'll share those techniques with you and explain how you can learn and apply them.

The trick is to store numbers as images. Your brain is much more proficient at storing images than it is at storing numbers or even words. I'm sure you can recall images from your childhood, like your favorite vacation spot. But numbers, or the exact words someone said to you? Not so much.

The first step in building a system that will allow you to store numbers effortlessly is to encode every number with a sound, as follows:

✓ 0–s
✓ 1–t
✓ 2–n
✓ 3–m
✓ 4–r
✓ 5–l
✓ 6–j/sh
✓ 7–k
✓ 8–v
✓ 9–b

Any other letters count as fillers and do not affect the number you're storing. With this encoded list in place, you can now turn any two-digit number into a word. For example, if you are trying to remember the number 42 you could form the word "rain."

There are a few things you can do with these encoded numbers:

- You can link them to words. For example, if you are trying to remember that Albert Einstein lived to be 76, you can form the word "kash" (remember this is about sounds not spelling), and then imagine Albert Einstein throwing dollar bills at a strip club.

- Or you can link them to more numbers. For example, if you are trying to remember the year 1802, all you have to do is link "TV" ("t" for 1 and "v" for 8) and "sun" ("s" for 0 and "n" for 2). To store the number, you could imagine watching TV and seeing the bright sun reflect from the screen.

In effect, you can remember as much information as you need in the form of a story.

As you can tell by my examples, the images and visuals will be pretty crazy. In fact, that is exactly what you want. The more vivid, outrageous, and personal an image, the easier it will be for you to remember. The brain is better at recalling unusual, sexual, or provocative things so don't be afraid to store some crazy images for better memory. Just make sure to always be logical in the connections you make. Don't choose words that can easily be confused with others.

The Major Memory System takes some training, but, once you master it, your ability to memorize numbers will improve dramatically. This system is best used for subjects like history, politics, and economics, where you have to link names to numbers, remember dates, and store very specific numbers.

SUMMARY

- Use the following steps to memorize information: engage with the information, repeat and practice, relate to existing knowledge, use visuals, and organize and support.

- Utilize outlines with lots of different colors and shapes to study for tests.

- Create visual markers to store vast amounts of information.

- Learn the Memory Palace system to remember a lot of images, dates, and places.

- Learn the Major Memory System to store numbers as images.

"**Order** and simplification are the first steps toward mastery of a subject."

—*Thomas Mann*

CHAPTER 17:
HOW TO WRITE IN COLLEGE

The bad news: you will have to write a lot of papers in college and there is no way around it. Almost every college class requires writing.

The good news: college writing is very simple, and anyone can learn to be good at it. You do not have to be a wordsmith. Just read this chapter and apply it.

Most students hate writing essays, and they are really bad at it. They simply start putting down whatever comes to mind until they reach the word minimum. It's a horrible idea to write like that. You will waste a lot of time, and you will get bad grades. Here's what you need to do instead:

PREPARATION

- **Understand:** Make sure you know exactly what is asked of you. Is it an analysis, your opinion, or a research paper? Read the assignment, talk to the teacher, and talk to classmates about what they are writing about; make sure you know exactly what's expected.

- **Brainstorm:** If it's a research assignment, hit the library, find five relevant books or articles, and skim through them for 15 minutes to get a solid overview of the subject. If it is a paper about a specific book, read the whole thing. If the assignment requires your opinion, take one page and write down everything you know about the subject and supplement it by skim reading a few articles on the subject.

- **Organize:** A good outline of your paper will make all the difference.

To prepare your essay you need to write down the question(s) the assignment is asking and the best one-sentence answer you can give to the question. This sentence is your thesis and the most crucial element of any college essay. Next, you need to decide on three subtopics of your thesis, each of which directly supports it. Finally, you need at least two to three examples or quotes for each of the three subtopics. Gather all of this information before starting the paper, unless you are writing a research paper. In that case, you should first write the intro to your essay, including the thesis and three subtopics. Then do research for the subtopics to find two to three sources for each. Then simply continue your essay with the body paragraphs and incorporate the sources.

Now you are ready to build your essay. The following is the structure I used to get A's on almost all of my college essays. Using it is as easy as taking the information you created during the previous step and plugging it into the following structure.

Introduction

1. Start your paper with a "hook." This is a broad, intriguing sentence that captures the reader's attention and sets the stage for the entire paper.

2. Expand on your hook in three to five sentences. If you think about this in terms of a movie, this part would be the trailer. It gives just enough away to pull the reader in.

3. Write your thesis. This sentence is critical. Review what your teacher is asking of you, and make sure you understand the question. Then find the best specific answer to that question, and phrase it in one sentence.

4. Come up with a single sentence that sums up the first body paragraph. This is the first of the three subtopics you found earlier during your preparation. This sentence is often called a mini-thesis, because it describes the point you will argue in the first paragraph.

5. Write the setup sentence for the second body paragraph (just like the sentence you just wrote).

6. Write the setup sentence for the third body paragraph (just like the two sentences before).

7. Form a transition sentence by restating your hook and thesis.

Body Paragraph #1

1. Rewrite the first paragraph's mini-thesis.

2. Support it with evidence and analysis using the two to three points and quotes you found earlier.

3. Restate your setup sentence by connecting it to your main thesis.

Body Paragraph #2

1. Rewrite the second paragraph's mini-thesis.

2. Support it with evidence and analysis using the two to three points and quotes you found earlier.

3. Restate your setup sentence by connecting it to your main thesis.

Body Paragraph #3

1. Rewrite the third paragraph's mini-thesis.

2. Support it with evidence and analysis using the two to three points and quotes you found earlier.

3. Restate your setup sentence by connecting it to your main thesis.

Conclusion

1. Restate your hook.

2. State your thesis one more time.

3. Write one to three sentences (depending on the length of your paper) to summarize the first body paragraph.

4. Add one to three sentences (depending on the length of your paper) to summarize the second body paragraph.

5. Write an additional one to three sentences (depending on the length of your paper) to summarize the third body paragraph.

6. Rewrite your hook and thesis into a conclusion sentence.

7. Finish by connecting your conclusion sentence to your hook. Just like the final scene of a good movie, this sentence should leave the reader thinking about life.

Notes and Advice

- Always present your strongest piece of evidence first.

- Use quotes only in your body paragraphs.

- When introducing quotes or points, move from broad to specific; end with a single analysis/conclusion sentence.

- Quotes can be as short as two to four words and should never exceed six to eight words. Always integrate your quote into an analysis sentence; never let the quote stand by itself.

How to Write

College writing is not about using fancy words, making art, or creating literature (unless you're an English major). It's about simplicity and structure. I learned everything I know about essay writing during my freshman year. I did not speak English well, struggled with grammar, and had a limited vocabulary. This forced me to develop very effective ways of writing. My essays were never beautiful, but they were well-structured and to the point. So if you can't write like Shakespeare, don't worry. It's entirely possible to get A's on every one of your college essays without a fancy vocabulary.

It might seem like a writing assignment is the right time to get creative, but, in most cases, that is a bad idea. For any subject other than creative writing, writing is just your means of conveying information. What matters is the content and the clarity with which you present it. Do not feel like you have to reinvent the wheel. Save your creativity for business, creative writing, and art. There is a time to be innovative, but your regular, everyday college essay is not it.

SUMMARY

- Plan your essays before you write them.
- Follow the template from this chapter for your essays unless your professor requests a specific format.
- Keep your writing simple and to the point.

"Research is what I'm doing when I don't know what I'm doing."

—*Wernher von Braun*

CHAPTER 18:
RESEARCH DONE RIGHT

For most people the term "research" awakens thoughts of hours upon hours in the library, browsing through books, journals, and innumerable websites. What a pain in the ass! And not at all what college-level research should be, if you are smart about it.

In my opinion, no one expects you to do really serious research during your undergrad years. Some professors might disagree with this statement, but I have found it to be true over and over again. Many professors will make it seem like research is hard and should take hours or even days. They will give you a personal tour of the library and a list of DOs and especially DON'Ts (stay away from Wikipedia and blogs) for utilizing online resources. Don't let them intimidate you or trick you into thinking you will have to spend a lifetime on your research paper. You won't. Here is what you should do instead:

> *Do not let the research dictate your writing; conduct specific research to support what you want to say.*

This obviously requires that you know what points you want to make before you start your research. Use the following steps to ensure that is the case:

1. Take 15 minutes to skim through a couple of articles and books to get an overview of the subject. Figure out what the goal of your essay is. Do not start specific research without a clear idea of what you want to say.

2. Write your introduction, including the thesis and the three thesis subtopics, using the steps listed in the previous chapter.

3. Find two sources for each of your three body paragraphs. They should be directly related to the mini-thesis of that body paragraph. Use mainly online publications: short articles with a clear headline by well-known and respected publications. Books are a time-killer; use them only if required by your teacher.

4. Don't be lazy; be effective. If your professor gives you specific instructions, follow them. If you're asked to read at least one book for your paper, speed-read it (learn how in the next chapter). Always be time-conscious; always remember the 80/20-principle. Never get caught up trying to find the perfect source for a point you want to make. Get it done and move on. Save author, publisher, book title, and website information for every source so you can easily implement the proper citation later.

5. Once you have enough sources, finish writing your body paragraphs and conclusion. Do not worry about the citations until the writing is completely done.

6. Once you finish writing, implement proper citation. Pay attention to details, so you do not lose any points. Most teachers are very specific on what citation style they want. Make sure you know their preference. Use the Purdue OWL Research and Citation website

(https://owl.english.purdue.edu/owl/section/2/) for a comprehensive overview of every style—MLA, APA, and CMS. Have your academic counselor or tutor check your paper to make sure the citations are correct.

SUMMARY

- When writing a research paper, first figure out what you want to say, and then find sources that support your points.

- Follow the research workflow outlined in this chapter to minimize time.

- Use the proper citations as requested by your professor and be sure to double-check them for accuracy.

"It is a skill that anyone can learn but it takes time to learn how to focus and to unlearn the way that we were all taught to read."

—*Anne Jones*
(Speed-reading champion who read
Go Set a Watchman *in 25½ minutes)*

CHAPTER 19:
SPEED-READING
FOR BEGINNERS

S peed-reading is not easy, but you should see some immediate results by implementing the techniques in this chapter. People who master speed-reading typically increase their wpm (words per minute) from about 220 to over 700, while increasing retention from 35 percent to 75 percent or more. It's possible to read at more than 1,000 wpm with 90 percent retention. However, reaching this level of skill will take a lot of time and practice.

Speed-readers make use of the following concepts:

- **Silent reading:** Most people read by vocalizing, meaning they hear every word in their head as they read it. As a result they read at close to the speed that they talk, instead of at the speed of their thoughts. Learning how to speed-read means shutting up the voice in your head and reading at the speed of your thoughts.

- **Saccades:** Instead of letting your eyes glide along the words, like most people do, speed-readers group words together and jump from one group to the next. These jumps are called saccades. The idea is to rapidly move your eyes from one fixation point to the next.

- **Varying speed:** You need to read at the right speed in order to maximize comprehension. The best speed-readers adjust their speed according to the content they're reading. They slow down whenever they encounter unfamiliar content or vocabulary, and they speed up when they can do so without missing anything important.

- **Prereading:** This means skimming through the chapter and section headlines to get an idea of the structure of the text before starting to read. It also allows you to set expectations and ask questions to improve your memory. Remember: engage with material before you read it.

- **Details over concepts:** As counterintuitive as it may seem, you have to learn to focus on the details (such as specific dates, names, and events) instead of general concepts of the text. The reason is simple: while you can always derive the general concepts and overarching ideas from the details, you can never derive a detail from the general concept. This is the key to higher retention during reading.

- **Marker Memory:** Your speed-reading skills are worth very little unless you are able to remember the information you consume. Scientifically speaking, decoding the information contained in a text is not enough. You have to then encode it and store it for later use. Remember the concept of markers we discussed in Chapter 16? It allows you to store the information in visual images while you speed-read. Ideally, you will create two to four markers for every paragraph, each encoded with three to five details. After every paragraph, you should take about 3 seconds to recall the visual markers you just created for the paragraph.

- **High concentration:** Speed-reading requires a much higher level of concentration than normal reading because you are doing three things at once: decoding, encoding, and storing information. In order to achieve the necessary level of concentration, you should turn off all distractions like your phone and laptop.

Become a Speed-Reader in Twelve Weeks

Week 1: Memory Basics

Speed-reading only works if your memory can keep up, so during the first phase of this program, you will increase your ability to visualize and store markers on the fly.

Play this short-term memory game once a day. Start with Level 1 and work your way up until you miss something. Play once a day until you fail.

http://neutralx0.net/home/mini04.html

Week 2: Visualization Basics

Look at an image for 10 seconds, then close your eyes and imagine it with as much detail as possible. Do at least five images a day.

http://pichost.me/

Week 3: Marker Basics

Use the following list to choose three words every day and create markers for them.

http://mnemonicdictionary.com/wordlist/GREwordlist

Then see what visuals others have come up with for the same words.

Weeks 4 and 5: Memory Advanced

Remember five images in order. Do this three times a day until you don't make any mistakes.

http://www.gamesforthebrain.com/game/masterpieces/

Use the following tool to generate twenty random images, and try to remember all of them. Place them in groups by color or meaning to improve your memory. Do two sets of twenty images every day.

http://www.keytostudy.com/random-images-generator/

Use the following tool to generate twenty random words and try to remember all of them. Try turning words into images or form short phrases or sentences to help you remember. Do two sets of twenty words every day.

http://www.keytostudy.com/20-random-words-generator/

Week 6: Linking Markers

Use the following tool to practice linking markers. Start with a list of three pairs, and add a pair every day until you reach your limit. Keep pushing yourself to remember more and more word pairs. Do this 15 minutes a day.

http://www.keytostudy.com/linking-markers-exercise/

Week 7: Speed-Reading Basics

The following tool will help you become better at multitasking, a skill essential to speed-reading. It trains your ability to keep track of numerous calculations at once. Start with two colors; then decrease the time while increasing the colors. Do this for 15 minutes every day.

http://www.keytostudy.com/multitasking-computations/

In order to see more words at once, you need to increase your peripheral vision. This will allow you to use fewer saccades per line.

http://www.keytostudy.com/visual-angle-training/

Weeks 8 and 9: Creating Markers While Reading

Use marker creation and visualization while you read for at least 30 minutes a day. The goal is not to be fast yet but to be accurate. Check yourself after each paragraph to see how many names and dates you remember. You should get to an average 90 percent retention rate before moving on to the next phase.

Week 10: Overload Speed-reading

The best way to get started is to use the overload method by reading at a speed far above your ability. Use three saccades per line for a normal size book. Actively move your eyes from one focus point to the next and have three focus points per line. You should really be pushing your speed at this stage, without worrying about comprehension. Try finishing each page in 10 seconds or less.

In addition, alternate the overload method with the genius tool available at www.spritzinc.com for 30 minutes every day. Spritz allows you to have text flash at you in single words, at speeds up to 1,000 wpm. Set the speed to at least 800 wpm, and try to understand as much as you can. At the end of each training section, try a lower setting of 400–600 wpm. It will seem slow and really easy in comparison.

Weeks 11 and 12: Master Speed-reading

The last step is to combine speed with accuracy. At this stage, you should be speed-reading for at least 30 minutes a day. Start every session with 3 minutes of Spritz, reading at a speed above your level of comprehension. Then speed-read a book or an online article for 12 minutes at a slightly lower speed that allows you to comprehend most of the material. Work on creating markers and recalling as much information after each paragraph as possible. Then repeat the process one more time, Spritz-reading for 3 minutes followed by 12 minutes of speed-reading at a more comfortable speed.

Notes and Advice

- Fewer saccades per line means faster reading. The step from three to two saccades means a significant jump in your reading speed. Focus on increasing your peripheral vision to see multiple words at once.

- The positioning of your saccades is crucial. If you start each line on the first word, you're losing time. Your first saccade should be on the fourth or fifth word of each line. Your peripheral vision will catch the words at the beginning. Similarly your last saccade should not have a focus point on the last word but rather a few of words before the end of each line.

- Do not neglect the memory part of speed-reading. It does not help you if you speed-read without being able to recall the information after.

- Consider doing some of the exercises mentioned previously while traveling, during breaks, or when you are bored. If you are killing time, you might as well get smarter in the process.

- If you are serious about speed-reading, I recommend the course "Become a SuperLearner 2: Learn Speed Reading & Boost Memory" on www.udemy.com, by Jonathan A. Levi, et al. It contains a vast amount of highly valuable advice, a community of supporters, and in-depth learning materials.

SUMMARY

- Eliminate distractions while reading.

- Pre-read the text and scan pages for headlines to understand the structure of the text.

- Move your eyes in saccades instead of gliding along the text.

- Remember details instead of broad concepts. You can always recreate the concepts later on if you remember enough details.

- Store details as visual markers.

- Utilize the overload principle when practicing speed-reading. Train for reading speed first and for comprehension and memory later.

AFTERWORD

Most of what I have accomplished thus far in life, I owe to basketball. The game has made me who I am. It has opened up doors I never thought possible, and it has led me to where I am today. We are products of our sport. Sadly, for most of us, that means a few years of glory, followed by decades of insignificance. Only a few understand that to go beyond athletics means to change your impact from 4 to 40 years or more. It takes hard work, but it is worth it. There are three essential truths contained within this book that I would like you to remember:

1. Your time on this earth is limited, and it's up to you to make the most of it.

2. As a student-athlete, you're in a privileged position; take advantage of it.

3. To achieve true greatness, you have to become more than just an athlete.

It's important to remember that success, achievement, and greatness are concepts defined by people, and, as such, mean different things to different people. A lot of money can mean success to one person, while having a child can mean success to another. It's your life, your story, so you get to define what your goals are and what success means for you. The key is to define it and to strive for it.

Finally, the realization that there is a life and a future beyond your sport is not about giving up on your dreams as an athlete. Just because there is only a 1 percent chance of going pro doesn't mean you can't do it. It's important that you believe in your dreams, and this book should never take that away from you. My hope, however, is that you learn to expand your dreams and passions to create an amazing life for yourself and the people around you, whether it's as an athlete or as a professional.

THANK YOU

This book would not have been possible without the support of my family and friends. My parents, Kathrin and Jochen, have been there for me all the way, supporting any decision I ever wanted to make. My brothers, Paul and Luis, are the ones I call for advice. A handful of friends I consider family have made this journey and, therefore, this book possible. Thanks to each of you.

ABOUT THE AUTHOR

Malte Kramer is a German-born student-athlete turned serial entrepreneur, speaker, and author. He's the founder and CEO of multiple companies including GIVVR, a unique fundraising and awareness platform for nonprofits, and Luxury Presence, a real estate technology company whose clients include some of the world's most successful real estate agents.

In 2010, Malte came to the United States to realize his childhood dream of playing college basketball. After two years at Cuesta College, he was recruited by Pepperdine University to play basketball on a full scholarship. In 2014, he graduated as the valedictorian of his class with a 4.0 GPA, earning multiple honors, including Academic All-American, WCC Scholar-Athlete, and Pepperdine Scholar-Athlete of the Year.

Malte frequently speaks at colleges and conferences and has been featured on various radio and TV shows and podcasts like "Business Rockstars."